GNOSIS
DIVINE WISDOM

By the same author:
The Transcendent Unity of Religions
Spiritual Perspectives and Human Facts
Language of the Self
Stations of Wisdom
Understanding Islam
Light on the Ancient Worlds
In the Tracks of Buddism
Dimensions of Islam
Logic and Transcendence
Islam and the Perennial Philosophy

GNOSIS
DIVINE WISDOM

Blessed is the man who has found wisdom ...
Her ways are good ways, and all her paths are peaceful,
She is a tree of life to all that lay hold upon her
Proverbs iii

Frithjof Schuon

Translated from the French
by G.E.H. Palmer

PERENNIAL BOOKS LTD
Pates Manor, Bedfont, Middlesex

First published in France under the title
'Sentiers de Gnose'
by Editions du Vieux Colombier
14 March 1957
First United Kingdom Edition 1959
Second Impression 1978

ISBN 0 900599 13 6

Made and printed in Great Britain

Contents

Translator's Foreword

Man's most fundamental needs can be summed up as the need for Knowledge, the need for Love and the need for a Way to salvation. That these three needs have many degrees and modes and that they are closely related to one another is obvious. But man's external conditions and inner state combine to make less and less possible a full satisfaction of these needs. As heterodoxy, science and materialism claim increasingly to dominate attention and values, so more and more people feel cut off from any true meaning of existence, and are forced to make search for some fundamental basis of living, such as they fail to find in the normal terms of their environment.

This search often leads in the direction of a study of oriental or mystical traditions; but a great number of those who feel impelled to this search have little or no guidance or discrimination to rely upon. In these conditions many are virtually helpless to reach any but the most tenuous conclusions and may indeed lose heart or go far astray.

For such people, the writings of Frithjof Schuon can provide assistance of great value; while for those who are already on some real Traditional Way they offer a source of wise and powerful counsel. For here is a writer who has an outstandingly clear view of the transcendent metaphysical truths underlying all the great Revelations embodied in the various Traditions now available to man, as well as a vivid understanding both of his spiritual necessities and of the widely differing conditions of their fulfilment, within man himself and within the differing frameworks of the various civilisations.

This rare combination of qualities, together with a power of forceful presentation of his themes, makes Frithjof Schuon one of the most significant spiritual influences in the western world today. Of the first of his books to be translated into English

T. S. Eliot wrote: 'I have met with no more impressive work, in the comparative study of Oriental and Occidental Religion, than *The Transcendent Unity of Religions*. Even those who cannot accept the author's conclusions must feel challenged by this book to produce an answer of their own.'

The book now translated was published in French as *Sentiers de Gnose*. The term 'gnosis' as used here has no connection with the historical doctrines known as 'gnosticism'. It keeps its original meaning of Wisdom made up of Knowledge and Sanctity. Many passages in this book, and more particularly the sixth chapter, 'Gnosis, Language of the Self', make clear the distinction, often nowadays obliterated, between knowledge acquired by the ordinary discursive mind and the higher Knowledge which comes of intuition by the Intellect, the term Intellect having the same sense as in Plotinus or Eckhart. This distinction is fundamental to an understanding of the author's writings.

In addition to *The Transcendent Unity of Religions* mentioned above, there is also available in English the author's *Spiritual Perspectives and Human Facts*; the present book carries a stage further his exposition not only of different aspects of the great Traditions, but also of the ways whereby some may attain to the Wisdom, Love and Sanctity which are the fruits of spiritual realisation, the possibility for which mankind may in a sense be said to exist. The book closes with a remarkable section on the Christian tradition, especially under its more intellectual aspects, relating it to the general perspective outlined above.

G.E.H.P.

CLEARING THE GROUND

I

The Sense of the Absolute
in Religions

Religions are cut off from one another by barriers of mutual incomprehension; one of the principal causes of this appears to be that the sense of the absolute stands on a different plane in each of them, so that what would seem to be points of comparison often prove not to be. Elements resembling one another in form appear in such diverse contexts that their function and their nature too changes, at any rate to some extent; and this is so because of the infinitude of the All-Possible, which excludes precise repetition. In short, the sufficient reason of a 'new'[1] phenomenon is, from the point of view of the manifestation of possibilities, its difference in relation to 'antecedent' phenomena.

Worlds are not made for one another, and the cause of their particularities is also that of their diversity, hence of their reciprocal exclusion; we might simply take note of this situation and leave each world to speak in its own language—without trying to show that this language is, precisely, one language among others—were it not that this diversity gives a pretext to those who wish to destroy the very idea of the absolute and the values attaching to it. We live in an age when the interpenetration of civilisations raises many problems, not new, it is true, but singularly 'actual' and 'urgent'; in order to confront a relativism which is growing ever more intrusive, it is necessary

[1] The frequent use of inverted commas in this book is due to the fact that expressions which are merely logical do not always keep step with spiritual reality—indeed this is far from being the case. It is also a fact that the meanings of many words have shrunk to some extent with usage, or else that they have come to suggest associations of ideas that are more less restrictive; nor should we forget that the modern reader has more difficulty in 'reading between the lines' than his predecessor of olden times, so that greater precision and more shades of meaning are necessary.

to restore to the intelligence a sense of the absolute, even to the point of having, for this very purpose, to underline the relativity which invests immutable things. We are thinking of the possibility, perhaps still far off, that the old religions might present a single front against the floodtide of materialism and pseudo-spiritualism; and knowing well that many sincere and fervent minds will not be disposed to accept all our theses, we hope none the less that—without apologising for our convictions and without wishing to address ourselves to everyone— we shall at least be able to open fresh horizons for them.

*

To give one example of the religious difficulties to which we are alluding, we would say that it seems quite natural to the Christian to generalise the 'structure' of his conviction which, in his case, results first from the divinity of Christ, and so from the signs that manifest this divinity, then from its power of salvation, and finally from the historical character of all these factors; basing himself exclusively on these criteria and not finding their exact equivalent elsewhere, the Christian will see nothing but improbability outside of his own spiritual cosmos. The Moslem will have the same feeling, but in favour of Islam and for a more or less inverse reason: whilst in Christianity the centre of religion is the 'Word made flesh', of which the Church is only the 'mystical body', in the Moslem climate it is Islam as such—the divine Law enveloping man and the whole of society —which is of prime importance; here it is a question of a 'totality' and not of a 'centre', and in actual fact the Prophet is not the determining centre from which all flows, but the personification of this totality; it is on the totality that the stress is put and not on the spokesman, and it is the divine quality of this totality—of this terrestrial crystallisation of the celestial Will[1]—with the inner experience flowing from the practice of his religion, which confer on the Moslem his profound con-

[1] This Will is in Islam conceived as 'divine Word' and 'uncreated Book' at one and the same time.

viction; and let us add that the Koran, while being the 'centre' or the 'christic' element of the religion, becomes its irresistible element only through the process of deployment—*el-islâm*; it then manifests itself as a system of channels divinely prepared to receive and direct the flow of the human will. While blessedness for the Christian is to cling to the saving divinity of Christ, even to share in His cross, blessedness for the Moslem on the contrary consists in being expanded in a totality, in 'surrendering' (*aslama*, whence the word *islâm*) his will to God, in 'abandoning' it in the mould of a divine Will which encompasses the whole human personality, from the body to the spirit, and from birth to the encounter with God.

And here is what is important: this system of sacred channels —or this divine schema which, 'seen from above', has the crystalline homogeneity of a large snowflake—this system confers on the human will a saving quality of unity, which it would by no means possess of itself and which it could acquire only through an act of mercy from the Most High. The first condition of this 'abandonment' of the self is a conforming of the intelligence to this unity: the first demand of '*el-islâm*' is the acceptance of the One God and of His saving Providence, 'the Prophets'. When this acceptance occurs on the plane of the Intellect, conviction results from metaphysical evidence; and in an analogous manner, each tradition comprises a 'mythological' evidence which flows, subjectively, from the mental dispositions of such and such a human receptacle, and, on a higher level, an intellectual evidence which derives from gnosis[1] and from the metaphysical and mystical transparency of symbols.

*

What we have said of Islam applies equally to Judaism; Islam is distinguished from Judaism by ethnical universality—which it has in common with Christianity—secondly by the simplicity and suppleness of its Law, and finally—or indeed above all—

[1] For the use of the word 'gnosis' see p. 8, above.

by the abrahamic 'climate' of its theism. If Christianity 'places God in man' through the mystery of the Incarnation, Judaism, in its turn, 'places man in God' through the mystery of the 'chosen People'; it is impossible to dissociate the God of the Jews from His people: who says Jehovah, says Israel, and conversely. The great Revelation of Monotheism—or the great personal manifestation of God—took place in Israel, and it is this 'fact', the mystery of Sinai, together with the choosing of this people, which gives to the believing Jew his unshakable conviction, and constitutes for him that 'element of the absolute' without which no religious faith is possible.

The great Messengers, if they are assuredly One by their principle, in their gnosis and in the Logos, are not however of necessity equal on the phenomenal plane, that of manifestation on earth; what are equivalent are the Messages, when each is taken in its entirety. It is necessary, in any case, not to confuse the phenomenal or the cosmic with the spiritual reality; it is the latter which is one, and it is the former which is diverse.[1]

*

For the Christian, the overwhelming argument is the divinity of Christ, and, flowing from this, the fact that there is an intermediary between God and man in the form of God made man, not to mention another intermediary, the Mother of God; but, if the argument of divinity presupposes that the value of the

---

[1] Hinduism distinguishes between 'full' and 'partial' *avatâras*: in the latter, only a 'fragment' of Divinity is incarnated. The Koran, whilst on the one hand affirming the principial unity of the Messengers, on the other hand admits differences of level or of 'favours', which means, for the Moslem commentators, that one Messenger can be superior to another in respect of some particular excellence. This mystery of human diversity within the avataric unity, or of the incommensurability between earthly manifestation and 'inner' or 'celestial reality', has given rise, in the Mahâyâna, to the doctrine of the 'three bodies of the Buddha': *nirmâna-kâya* is the human form of the Blessed One; *sambhoga-kâya* is His celestial and glorious being; *dharma-kâya* is His absolute reality, the Buddha *in divinis*, as Logos.

Message should be made to depend on this divinity, the argument of proximity presupposes that God is remote, which is clearly true in a certain respect, but not in every respect. Islam starts precisely from the idea that the infinitely transcendent God is at the same time infinitely close—'closer than your jugular artery'—so that in religious experience He surrounds us and penetrates us, like a sort of luminous ether, if one may use such an imaginative expression; the only necessary intermediary is our own attitude, *el-islâm*, the central element of which is prayer in all its forms.

The Judaic God is 'remote', but He dwells among His people and sometimes speaks to them; the Christian God—as Man-God —is the 'intermediary' between this remote God and man, this God who is thenceforth silent and merciful; and as for the God of Islam, He is, for His part, 'near' (*El-Qarîb*) without being 'human'. These are not different Gods, of course; it is solely a question of different perspectives, and of 'divine attitudes' corresponding to them respectively. God is always and everywhere God, and that is why each of these attitudes is to be found after its own mode, in the heart of the other two; there is always, in one mode or another, both 'remoteness' and 'proximity', as there is always an 'intermediary' element.

*

The 'sense of the absolute' is not grafted exactly on the same organic element, as between one religion and another—whence the impossibility of making comparisons between the elements of religions simply from the outside—and this fact is shown clearly by the differing natures of conversions to Christianity and to Islam: while conversion to Christianity seems in certain respects like the beginning of a great love, which makes all a man's past life look vain and trivial—it is a 'rebirth' after a 'death'—conversion to Islam is on the contrary like awakening from an unhappy love, or like sobriety after drunkenness, or again like the freshness of morning after a troubled night. In

Christianity, the soul is 'freezing to death' in its congenital egoism, and Christ is the central fire which warms and restores it to life; in Islam, on the other hand, the soul is 'suffocating' in the constriction of the same egoism, and Islam appears as the cool immensity of space which allows it to 'breathe' and to 'expand' towards the boundless. The 'central fire' is denoted by the cross; the 'immensity of space' by the Kaaba, the prayer-rug, the abstract interlacings of Islamic art.

In a word, the faith of the Christian is a 'concentration', and that of the Moslem an 'expansion' (*bust, inshirâh*) as the Koran moreover states[1]; but each of these 'modes' is of necessity to be found somewhere within the framework of the 'opposing' perspective. 'Concentration' or 'warmth' reappears in Sufic 'love' (*mahabbah*), whilst 'expansion' or 'coolness' penetrates into Christian gnosis, and in a more general way into the 'peace of Christ', as the basis of 'purity of heart' and contemplation.

*

To pass from one Asiatic tradition—Hinduism, Buddhism or Taoism—to another is in effect no great matter, seeing that the metaphysical content is everywhere quite apparent and even emphasises the relative nature of the diversities in the various 'mythologies'; these traditions—precisely because of their spiritual transparency—readily absorb elements of foreign traditions; the Shinto divinity becomes a *bodhisattva*, without change of essence, since the names cover universal realities. But inside the framework of the three Semitic traditions, a change of religion almost amounts to a change of planet, for within this framework the divergent 'alchemical positions' have

---

[1] 'Have not We (God) expanded (or 'opened') thy breast (O Mohammed) and removed the burden which weighed on thy back?' (Surat: 'Have We not expanded?' 1, 2 and 3). Again: 'He whom God desires to guide, He expands his breast for Islam, and he whom He desires to stray, He constricts his breast and shrinks it . . .' (Surat of the Cattle, 125).

to be supported on one and the same prophetic and messianic Monotheism, so that the particular form engrosses the whole man; spiritual 'keys' present themselves as exclusive 'facts', for otherwise they risk becoming inoperative; gnosis alone has the right to be aware that a key is a key.[1]

Metaphysical evidence has precedence over 'physical' or 'phenomenal' certainty in cases where such a question can arise; moreover, certainty on this latter level could never weaken or abolish the self-evidence of the principles, eternal 'thoughts' of God.

*

The differences between religions are reflected very exactly in different sacred arts: compared with Gothic art, and above all the 'flamboyant' style, Islamic art is contemplative rather than

[1] When one looks closely at the intentions hidden behind the verbal formulations, one perceives that the apparent rejection of the divinity of Christ by Islam signifies, not that the perspective of unity denies such a fundamental reality, but that its intellectual structure excludes the Christian formulation; in other words, Islam splits in two the personality of the Man-God, according to the levels to which the two natures belong, and it does so because it envisages Being only in its extra-cosmic divinity. This perspective, which cannot fail to take a dogmatic turn, aims at the same time at avoiding the danger of the *de facto* 'divinising' of the human individual, that is to say the danger of individualist 'humanism' with all its consequences; there is here as it were a rebound from 'deification'.—From the Moslem point of view the saying of Christ: 'Before Abraham was, I am' signifies that the Logos, the uncreated 'Word' of God, and consequently the Intellect as such, 'precedes' principially all temporal, even prophetic and primordial manifestation.—As for the apparent denial of the crucifixion by the Koran, we have always held that this is a question of theology rather than of history, and we have met the same point of view in a work of Louis Massignon (*Le Christ dans les Evangiles selon Al-Ghazâlî*): '. . . Abu Hatim, basing himself on the opinion of one of his masters (who is not named), declares that the beginning of the Koranic verse (IV, 156) in no way denies the crucifixion, and that it must be interpreted after taking account of its ending: "and they did not kill him truly (*yaqînâ*), God raised him to Himself", and, since Jesus died a martyr, recollecting the verses (II, 149: cf. III, 163) on the death of martyrs: "Do not say of those who have been killed on the way of God that they are dead: but that they are living; although you are not aware of it." '

volitive: it is 'intellectual' and not 'dramatic', and it opposes the cold beauty of geometrical design to the mystical heroism of cathedrals. Islam is the perspective of omnipresence ('God is everywhere'), which coincides with that of 'simultaneity' ('Truth has always been'); it aims at avoiding any 'particularisation' or 'condensation', any 'unique fact' in time and in space, although, as a religion, it necessarily comprises an aspect of 'unique fact', on pain of ineffectiveness or even of absurdity. In other words, Islam aims at what is 'centre everywhere', and that is why, symbolically speaking, it replaces the cross with the cube or the woven fabric: it 'decentralises' and 'universalises' to the greatest possible extent in the realm of art as in that of doctrine; it is opposed to any individualist node and so to any 'personalist' mysticism.

To express ourselves in geometrical terms, we will say that a point, which seeks to be unique and would thus become an absolute centre, appears to Islam—in art as in theology—as a usurpation of the divine absoluteness and therefore as an 'association' (*shirk*); there is only one single centre, God, whence the prohibition of images that 'centralise', especially statues; even the Prophet, the human centre of the tradition, has no right to a 'uniqueness' like that of Christ and is precluded from this by the emphasis laid on the series of the other Prophets; the same is true of Islam—or the Koran—which is similarly integrated in a universal 'fabric' and a cosmic 'rhythm', since it has been preceded by other religions—or 'Books'— which it merely restores. The *Kaaba*, centre of the Moslem world, becomes space as soon as one is in the interior of the building: the ritual direction of prayer is then projected towards the four cardinal points. If Christianity is like a central fire, Islam on the contrary resembles a sheet of snow, unifying and levelling at the same time, and having its centre everywhere.

*

There is, in every religion, not only a choice for the will between the beyond and the here-below, but also a choice for the intelligence between truth and error; there are however differences of correlation, in the sense that Christ is true because He is the Saviour—whence the importance that the phenomenal element assumes here—whilst when Islam has salvation in view it starts from a discrimination which is in the last analysis metaphysical (*lâ ilaha illâ 'Llâh*), and it is this Truth which saves; but whether it is a question of Christianity or of Islam or of any other traditional form, it is indeed the metaphysical truth which, thanks to its universality, determines the values of things. And as this truth envelops and penetrates all, there is in it neither 'here-below' nor 'beyond', nor any choice by the will; only the universal essences count, and these are 'everywhere and nowhere'; there is, on this plane, no choice for the will to make, for, as Aristotle says, 'the soul is all that it knows'. This contemplative serenity appears in the abstract freshness of mosques as also in many Romanesque churches and in certain elements of the best Gothic, particularly in the rose windows, which are like 'mirrors of gnosis' in these sanctuaries of love.

May we here be permitted, at the risk of repetition, to return again to certain parallelisms: if Christianity can be at least partially defined with the help of the words 'miracle', 'love', 'suffering', Islam, in its turn, will correspond to the triad 'truth', 'force', 'poverty'; Islamic piety makes one think less of a 'centre' filled with a sweet and vivifying warmth—the Christian form of *barakah*—than of a 'present' in a white, fresh light; its spiritual means are dynamic rather than affective, although the differences, in this realm, are doubtless far from absolute. Moslem asceticism has about it something dry and of the desert, possessing scarcely any of the dramatic attraction of the asceticism of the West; but in its climate of patriarchal poverty there is a musical and lyrical element which recreates the Christian climate on a different basis.

We said above that Islam has a bias towards basing itself on the element 'Truth'—that is to say that it puts the accent there according to its own point of view and its own aims—and that

it is the 'impersonal' character of this element which 'decentralises' Islamic 'mythology'. In Christianity it will doubtless be
considered that the 'divine Reality'—manifested by Christ—
has precedence over 'truth', the former being 'concrete' and
the second 'abstract', which is the case when 'truth' is reduced
to the level of thought; but we must not lose sight of the fact
that we have *a priori* no knowledge of the divine Reality in the
absence of metaphysical truth, whatever may be the degree of
our understanding; from another angle, the word 'truth' is often
taken as synonymous with 'reality'—'I am the way, the truth
and the life'—and this is how Islam takes it. It is precisely
because to start with we have no knowledge going beyond the
'truth', that we have a right to call 'true' what is 'real', a terminology which in no way prejudices the effective—and eventually
'concrete'—quality of our apparently 'abstract' knowledge. In
any case, the 'subjective' manifestation of the Absolute is no
less real than its 'objective' manifestation; certitude is itself a
miracle.

*

A question which inevitably arises here is that of the historicity of the great phenomena of the religions: ought more
confidence to be placed in that tradition which presents a
maximum of historical evidence? To this the reply must be that
there is no metaphysical or spiritual difference between a truth
manifested by temporal facts and a truth expressed by other
symbols, under a mythological form for example; the modes of
manifestation correspond to the mental requirements of the
different groups of humanity. If certain mentalities prefer
marvels that are empirically 'improbable' to historical 'reality',
that is precisely because the marvellous—with which in any
case no religion could dispense—indicates transcendence in
relation to terrestrial facts; we are tempted to say that the aspect
of improbability is the sufficient reason for the marvellous, and
it is this unconscious need for feeling the essence of things

which explains the tendency to exaggerate found among certain peoples: it is a trace of nostalgia for the Infinite. Miracles denote an interference of the marvellous in the sensory realm; whoever admits miracles must also admit the principle of the marvellous as such, and even tolerate pious exaggeration on a certain plane. The opportuneness of 'mythological' marvels on the one hand and the existence of contradictions between religions on the other—which do not imply any intrinsic absurdity within the bounds of a given religion, any more than the internal contradictions found in all religions are absurd—these factors, we say, show in their own way that, with God, the truth is above all in the symbol's effective power of illumination and not in its literalness, and that is all the more evident since God, whose wisdom goes beyond all words, puts multiple meanings into a single expression[1]; an obscurity in expression—whether elliptical or contradictory—often indicates a richness or a depth in meaning, and this it is which explains the apparent incoherences to be found in the sacred Scriptures. God manifests in this way His transcendence in relation to the limitations of human logic; human language can be divine only in an indirect way, neither our words nor our logic being at the height of the divine purpose. The uncreated Word shatters created speech, whilst at the same time directing it towards concrete and saving truth.

Must the conclusion of all this then be that from the point of view of spirituality an historical basis has in itself less value than a mythological or purely metaphysical basis, on the grounds that principles are more important than phenomena? Assuredly not, in so far as it is a question of symbolism; what has less value is an attribution to this historical basis of a significance greater than it should have, a substituting of it for the symbolic truth and the metaphysical reality it expresses; none the less the importance of historical fact remains intact in respect of sacred

---

[1] Just as the blow of a hammer produces a multitude of sparks, so, say the Kabbalists, a single word of the Torah comprises multiple meanings.

institutions. From another point of view, it should be noted that a traditional narrative is always true; the more or less mythical features which are imposed on the historical life of the Buddha, for instance, are so many ways of expressing spiritual realities which it would be difficult to express otherwise.[1] In cases where Revelation is most expressly founded on history, and to the extent that this is so, the historical mode is no doubt necessary: in a world which was heir to Jewish 'historicism' and to Aristotelian empiricism, Revelation could not fail to take wholly the form of an earthly event, without the adjunction of any non-historical symbolism; but we must observe that a too great insistence on historicity—not historicity as such—may somewhat obscure the metaphysical content of sacred facts, or their spiritual 'translucency', and can even end, in the form of abusive criticism, by 'eroding' history itself and by belittling what is too big for man's powers of conception.[2]

Those who favour rigorous historicity against the mythologies of Asia will doubtless object that the historical truth furnishes proofs of the validity of the means of grace: in this context, it is

[1] The fact that the life of the Buddha, which is historical in its main features, including certain miracles, retraces the myth of Indra, in no way means that it is itself a myth, any more than the prophecies concerning Christ invalidate His historical reality. On the contrary, if the first steps of the Buddha after the Illumination were marked by lotuses, this fact belongs to the subtle order; it is not in any way 'unreal'.

[2] The deliberate vilification of the Holy Virgin carried on by Péguy and many others, is one example of this kind of thing. Another example is the 'criticism', not only 'archaeological', but even 'psychological', of sacred facts, a distortion which is at the opposite pole from intellectuality and excludes understanding of the facts in question. Modern exegesis is only a caricature of ancient hermeneutics, if indeed there is still any relationship between them; it consists above all of giving doubts and prejudices the status of dogmas: according to these prejudices, it is 'impossible' that a book should be prior to a certain date, or that a scribe should have copied a book, even a sacred one, without altering it; quite improper conclusions are drawn from the smallest facts and the most disproportionate deductions and inductions are allowed, though all the positive data are contrary to these false principles.

necessary to point out, firstly that historical proofs, precisely, could not be quite rigorous in this realm, and secondly that tradition as such, with all that it comprises in the way of symbolism, doctrine and sanctity—not to mention other more or less indeterminate criteria—furnishes much more unexceptionable proofs of the divine origin and the validity of rites; in a sense, the acceptance by tradition—and the development in sanctity—of a means of grace is a criterion far more convincing than historicity, not to mention the intrinsic value of the Scriptures. History is often incapable of verification; it is tradition, not criticism, which guarantees it, but it guarantees at the same time the validity of non-historical symbolisms. It is the actual and permanent miracle of tradition which nullifies the objection that no man living has been a witness of sacred history; the saints are its witnesses in quite other fashion than the historians; to deny tradition as the guarantee of truth amounts in the end to asserting that there are effects without causes.

There is, doubtless, no truth more 'exact' than that of history; but what must be stressed is that there is a truth more 'real' than that of facts; the higher reality embraces the 'exactness', but the latter, on the contrary, is far from presupposing the former. Historical reality is less 'real' than the profound truth it expresses and which myths likewise express; a mythological symbolism is infinitely more 'true' than a fact deprived of symbolism. And that brings us back to what we were saying above, namely that the mythological or historical opportuneness of the marvellous, as also the existence of dogmatic antinomies, go to show that for God truth is above all in the efficacy of the symbol and not in the 'bare fact'.

From the point of view of historicity or of its absence, three degrees must be distinguished: mythology, qualified historicity and exact historicity. We find the first degree in all mythology properly so called, as also in the monotheistic accounts of the creation, and the second degree in the other 'prehistoric' narratives, whether they concern Noah or Jonah or the human

avatâras of Vishnu[1]. In Judaism, rigorous historicity starts
perhaps at Sinai; in Christianity, it appears in the whole of the
New Testament,[2] but not in the Apocrypha or the Golden
Legend, which moreover are not canonical works, a fact that
has earned them a quite undeserved disregard, since symbolism
is an essential vehicle of truth; lastly, in Islam, exact historicity
attaches to the life of the Prophet and of his Companions, as
well as to those of their sayings (*ahâdith*) recognised by the
tradition,[3] but not to the stories concerning the pre-Islamic

[1] The non-human *avatâras* belong, in our opinion, to mythological
symbolism; all the same it is necessary to avoid putting into this
category all the phenomena which contradict the experience of our
millennium. On this score we should like to remark that we see no
logical reason for denying historicity to the loves of the *gopis*, for if
such a symbolism be possible, it has also the right to exist on the plane
of facts; there is something analogous in the case of the 'Song of Songs',
where the literal meaning keeps all its rights, since it exists; moral
interest must not be confused with the truth which runs through all
levels of Existence.

[2] Let us notice all the same the existence of a certain variability, for
example on the subject of the 'three Mary Magdalenes', as also some
contradictory features in the Gospel stories, which seem to us to
indicate that sacred things, while being situated here in time, are
beyond history; such 'irregularities' are in no way contrary to the
divine Will, and they are moreover to be found also in sacred art,
where they are like 'openings' safeguarding the indefinite flux of 'life';
this amounts to saying that every form is inadequate in the eyes of
Heaven. There is something of this also in the extreme freedom of
scriptural quotations in the New Testament: the divine Utterance,
in crystallising itself, rejects at the same time certain 'fixations'.—
Simply to read the Gospels is enough, from our point of view, to
reduce to nothing all the artificial arguments aimed at ruining the
authenticity of the texts. Those who, contrary to tradition, extol the
value of 'criticism' or of 'objective analysis', forget the essential,
namely intelligence, without which the best of methods is futile;
though indeed intelligence is often identified with a critical attitude, as if
to doubt evidence were a sufficient proof of being intelligent.

[3] According to a very widespread opinion, almost all the sayings
and gestures of the Prophet recorded by the Sunna are falsifications
produced by certain interested theologians. The psychological
improbability of such an hypothesis is ignored, and it seems to be
forgotten that the supposed falsifiers were men who believed in Islam
and feared hell; no weight is given to tradition or to orthodox

Prophets and events, which are woven of symbols certainly 'exact' but more or less 'mythical'; to take them literally however is always to let oneself be inspired by their 'alchemical' virtue, even when a real understanding is lacking.[1]

The historical perspective, with all its importance for a certain level of Christian doctrine, is however legitimate only in so far as it can be included in Platonic non-historicity. Christian 'personalism' derives from the fact of the Incarnation, and then from the 'bhaktic' character of Christianity, a character which in no way prevents this religion from 'containing' metaphysics and gnosis, for Christ is 'Light of the world'; but gnosis is not for everyone, and a religion cannot be metaphysical in its actual form; on the other hand, Platonism, which is not a religion, can be so. Christian 'historicity' which is conjoint with Jewish 'historicity', implies then no superiority in relation to other perspectives, nor any inferiority so long as the characteristic in question is situated at the level to which it rightfully belongs.

*

Does the object of faith have precedence over faith itself, or does faith have precedence over its object? Normally, it is the object which has precedence over faith, since it is what determines faith and provides it with sufficient reason; but from a

unanimity, of course, and this shows ignorance of what is possible in a tradition and what is not; basically it shows ignorance of what tradition is. If the Arab mentality is too scrupulous to accept a *hâdîth* without knowing the chain of its reporters (*isnâd*), still less would its scruples allow it to forge false texts; to pretend the contrary is to admit that there are men who risk damnation by piety. 'Woe to them for what their hand has written' says the Koran (II, 79). The fact that Moslem traditionalists started quite early to denounce certain falsifications only confirms what has just been said.

[1] The shock that the Christian suffers from the Koranic version of Bible stories in no way differs from the shock experienced by the Jew in face of the New Testament quotations of the Prophets, not to mention the strange forgetfulness, by Christians, of the Jewish exegesis, though this is really essential for proper comprehension of the Old Testament and could fill many gaps.

certain point of view and in certain cases, faith can be more important than its content and can 'force' the gates of Heaven despite the insufficiency of some immediate object of belief. Faith comprises two 'poles', one objective and dogmatic and the other subjective and mystical; the ideal is a perfect faith in an orthodox truth. It is idea which engenders faith, and the quality of the first determines the quality of the second, but the often paradoxical and unforeseeable play of universal Possibility can allow the predominance of the pole 'faith' over the pole 'idea', so that the Tibetans have been able to say that a dog's tooth which is mistaken for a relic and becomes the object of a sincere and ardent faith actually begins to shine.[1] There can in fact be a faith which, in its very substance, carries the imprint of a truth of which ordinary consciousness is more or less unaware, provided no intrinsic error compromises the quality of its ardour, which must be of such purity and nobility as will safeguard it from serious errors; such faith is like an 'existential' intuition of its 'intellectual' object. This possibility of a faith which excels the 'ideological' element and which 'compels' it, as it were, to surrender the truth in the end, presupposes a highly contemplative mentality, already freed from many obstacles; furthermore, if the quality of the faith can thus compensate for the precariousness of the idea, this idea must appear like a light, however feeble, and not like a darkness; on this plane there are many imponderables.

It is easy to understand the slight respect shown by *bhaktas*, or by some of them, for 'word for word' exactness in belief or cult if one takes into consideration their 'subjectivism'—we do not say their 'individualism'—which finds all the criteria of 'truth' in the intensity of faith and in the negation of the *ego*; it is true that such an attitude is not easily to be realised in just any kind of traditional climate, unless, apart from all

[1] The story is told of Vâlmîki that, invoking the divine name of Rama backwards (making it into *Mara*, the Evil One), he was saved by his faith. The exaggerated character of this story underlines its intention.

questions of doctrine, one has in mind those simple souls who devote a touching and efficacious cult to some pious image, and who are to be found *sub omni coelo*. We certainly do not wish to confuse naivety with intrinsic heresy, even when passive, although from the point of view of pure truth every limited concept has a provisional aspect of heresy; all we mean to say here is, not that error as such can be right, but that the *de facto* supremacy of a certain magic of the soul over correctness of the symbol exists by virtue of the 'exception which proves the rule', and that account must be taken of it if one wishes to grasp every aspect of the eternal traffic between man and God. Here we have a possibility which perhaps concerns men themselves less than the manner in which God sees and judges them. It is the whole mystery of the 'faith which removes mountains' and which 'saves', whatever may be our ignorance. A certain reversal of the normal polarity of faith is moreover to be found in all genuine faith, when it happens that the object of faith appears at the outset as 'dead letter'; but in this case, precisely, the normal relationships of things are not affected, for the symbol to be assimilated keeps all its value.

*

It remains for us to say some words on gnosis or the '*philo-sophia perennis*', which is the connecting link between the different religious languages. The mode of manifestation of gnosis is 'vertical' and more or less 'discontinuous'; it is like fire and not water, in the sense that fire arises from the invisible and can disappear into it again,[1] whereas water has a continuous existence; but the sacred Scriptures remain the necessary and unchanging basis, the source of inspiration and the criterion of all gnosis.[2] Direct and supra-mental intellection is in reality a

[1] *Zen*, with its 'a-doctrinal' character, is particularly representative of this aspect of gnosis.

[2] It is said, in Judaism, that esotericism was revealed by God to Moses in the Tabernacle and that it was lost subsequently, but that wise men were able to reconstitute it, basing themselves on the Torah. —Whatever may have been the diverse formulations of Christian

'remembering' and not an 'acquisition': intelligence, in this realm, does not take cognisance of something situated in principle outside itself, but all possible knowledge is on the contrary contained in the luminous substance of the Intellect—which is identified with the Logos by 'filiation of essence'— so that the 'remembering' is nothing other than an actualisation, thanks to an occasional external cause, or to an internal inspiration, of an eternal potentiality of the intellective substance. Discernment exists only in relation to the relative, even if it lies beyond creation and at the very level of Being, and it is that which explains why the Intellect has been compared to deep sleep—but a sleep eminently non-passive and supra-conscious—untroubled by dreams; the Intellect coincides, in its innermost nature, with the very Being of things[1]; and that is why gnosis shows the profound continuity between the diverse forms of consciousness of the absolute.

And why this consciousness, some will ask? Because the truth alone makes free; or better still: because there is no 'why' in respect of the truth, for it is our intelligence, our freedom, our very being; if it be not, we are not.

gnosis, the pneumatological mysteries always find their scriptural basis in the New Testament, notably in the prologue to St. John's Gospel and in the talk by night with Nicodemus, and also in the Epistles.—From the point of view of 'eternal life', there are certainly no 'second zone' faithful; however, 'in my Father's house are many mansions'; equality before God concerns the 'external' fact of salvation and not its possible 'internal' modes.

[1] It is in this sense that the Gospel can say of the Word which is Light—the divine Intellect—that 'All things were made by him; and without him was not anything made that was made' (John i, 3). See p. 8, above.

2

Diversity of Revelation

Seeing that there is but one Truth, must we not conclude that there is but one Revelation, one sole Tradition possible? To this our answer is, first of all, that Truth and Revelation are not absolutely equivalent terms, since Truth is situated beyond forms, whereas Revelation, or the Tradition which derives from it, belongs to the formal order, and that indeed by definition; but to speak of form is to speak of diversity, and so of plurality; the grounds for the existence and nature of form are: expression, limitation, differentiation. What enters into form, thereby enters also into number, hence into repetition and diversity; the formal principle—inspired by the infinity of the divine Possibility—confers diversity on this repetition. One could conceive, it is true, that there might be only one Revelation or Tradition for this our human world and that diversity should be realised through other worlds, unknown by man or even unknowable by him; but that would imply a failure to understand that what determines the difference among forms of Truth is the difference among human receptacles. For thousands of years already, humanity has been divided into several fundamentally different branches, which constitute so many complete humanities, more or less closed in on themselves; the existence of spiritual receptacles so different and so original demands differentiated refractions of the one Truth. Let us note that this is not always a question of race, but more often of human groups, very diverse perhaps, but none the less subject to mental conditions which, taken as a whole, make of them sufficiently homogeneous spiritual recipients; though this fact does not prevent some individuals from being able to leave their framework, for the human collectivity never has anything absolute about it. This being so, it can be said that the diverse Revelations do not really contradict one another, since they do not apply to the same receptacle, and since God never addresses the same message to two or more receptacles of divergent character, corresponding analogically, that is, to dimensions which are formally incompatible; contradictions arise only on one and the same level. The apparent antinomies between Traditions are like differences of language or of symbol; contradictions are in human receptacles, not in God; the diversity in the world is a function of its remoteness from the divine Principle, which amounts to saying that the Creator cannot will both that the world should be, and that it should not be the world.

If Revelations more or less exclude one another, this is so of necessity because God, when He speaks, expresses Himself in absolute mode; but this absoluteness relates to the universal content rather than to the form; it applies to the latter only in a relative and symbolical sense, because the form is a symbol of the content and so too of humanity as a whole, to which this content is, precisely, addressed. It cannot be that God should compare the diverse Revelations from outside as might a scholar; He keeps Himself so to speak at the centre of each Revelation, as if it were the only one. Revelation speaks an absolute language, because God is absolute, not because the form is; in other words, the absoluteness of the Revelation is absolute in itself, but relative *qua* form.

The language of the sacred Scriptures is divine, but at the same time it is necessarily the language of men; it is made for men and could be divine only in an indirect manner. This incommensurability between God and our means of expression is clear in the Scriptures, where neither our words, nor our logic are adequate to the celestial intention; the language of mortals does not *a priori* envisage things *sub specie aeternitatis*. The uncreated Word shatters created speech while directing it towards the Truth; it manifests thus its transcendence in relation to the limitations of human powers of logic; man must be able to overstep these limits if he wishes to attain the divine meaning of the words, and he oversteps them in metaphysical knowledge, the fruit of pure intellection, and in a certain fashion also in love, when he touches the essences. To wish to reduce divine Truth to the conditionings of earthly truth is to forget that there is no common measure between the finite and the Infinite.

The absoluteness of a Revelation demands its unicity; but on the level of facts such unicity cannot occur to the extent of a fact being produced that is unique of its kind, that is to say constituting on its own what amounts to a whole genus. Reality alone is unique, on whatever level it is envisaged: God, universal Substance, divine Spirit immanent in this Substance; however, there are 'relatively unique' facts, Revelation for example, for since all is relative and since even principles must suffer impairment, at any rate in appearance, and in so far as they enter into contingencies, uniqueness must be able to occur on the plane of facts; if unique facts did not exist in any fashion, diversity would be absolute, which is contradiction pure and simple. The two must both be capable of manifesting themselves, unicity as well as diversity; but the two manifestations are of necessity relative, the one must limit the other. It results from this, on the one hand that diversity could not abolish the unity which is its substance, and on the other that unity or unicity must be contradicted by diversity on its own plane of existence; in other words, in every manifestation of unicity, compensatory diversity must be maintained, and indeed a unique fact occurs only in a part and not in the whole of a cosmos. It could be said that such and such a fact is unique in so far as it represents God for such and such an environment, but not in so far as it exists; this existing however does not abolish the symbolism of the fact, it repeats it outside the framework, within which the unique fact occurred, but on the same plane. Existence, which conveys the divine Word, does not abolish the unicity of such and such a Revelation in its providentially appointed field, but it repeats the manifestation of the Word outside this field; it is thus that diversity, without abolishing the metaphysically necessary manifestation of unicity, none the less contradicts it outside a particular framework, but on the same level, in order thus to show that the uncreated and non-manifested Word alone possesses absolute unicity.

If the objection is raised that at the moment when a Revelation occurs, it is none the less unique for the world, and not for a part of the world only, the answer is that diversity does not necessarily occur in simultaneity, it extends also to the temporal succession, and this is clearly the case when it is a question of Revelations. Moreover, a uniqueness of fact must not be confused with a uniqueness of principle; we do not deny the possibility of a fact unique to the world in a certain period, but that of a fact unique in an absolute sense. A fact which appears unique in space, is not so in time, and inversely; but even within each of these conditions of existence, it could never be affirmed that a fact is unique of its kind—for it is the genus or the quality, not the particularity, which is in question—because we can measure neither time nor space, and still less other modes which elude us.

This whole doctrine is clearly illustrated by the following example: the sun is unique in our solar system, but it is not so in space; we can see other suns, since they are situated in space like ours, but we do not see them as suns. The uniqueness of our sun is belied by the multiplicity of the fixed stars, without thereby ceasing to be valid within the system which is ours under Providence; the unicity is then manifested in the part, not in the totality, although this part is an image of the totality and represents it for us; it then 'is', by the divine Will, the totality, but only for us, and only in so far as our mind, whose scope is likewise willed by God, does not go beyond forms; but even in this case, the part 'is' totality so far as its spiritual efficacy is concerned.

*

We observe the existence, on earth, of diverse races, whose differences are 'valid' since there are no 'false' as opposed to 'true' races; we observe also the existence of multiple languages, and no one thinks of contesting their legitimacy; the same holds good for the sciences and the arts. Now it would be astonishing if this diversity did not occur also on the religious plane, that is to say if the diversity of human receptacles did not involve diversity of the divine contents, from the point of view of form, not of essence. But just as man appears, in the framework of each race, simply as 'man' and not as a 'White' or a 'Yellow', and as each language appears in its own sphere as 'language' and not as such and such a language among others, so each religion is of necessity on its own plane 'religion', without any comparison or relative connotation which, in view of the end to be attained, would be meaningless; to say 'religion' is to say 'unique religion'; explicitly to practise one religion, is implicitly to practise them all.

An idea or an enterprise which comes up against insurmountable obstacles is contrary to the nature of things; the ethnic diversity of humanity and the geographical extent of the earth suffice to make highly unlikely the axiom of one unique religion for all men, and on the contrary highly likely—to say the least—the need for a plurality of religions; in other words, the idea of a single religion does not escape contradiction if one takes account of its claims to absoluteness and universality on the one hand, and the psychological and physical impossibility of their realisation on the other, not to mention the antinomy between such claims and the necessarily relative character of all religious mythology; only pure metaphysic and pure prayer are absolute and therefore universal. As for 'mythology', it is—apart from its intrinsic content of truth and efficacy—indispensable for enabling metaphysical and essential truth to 'gain a footing' in such and such a human collectivity.

Religion is a 'supernaturally natural' fact which proves its truth—from the point of view of extrinsic proofs—by its human universality, so that the plurality and ubiquity of the religious phenomenon constitutes a powerful argument in favour of religion as such. Just as a plant makes no mistake in turning towards the light, so man makes no mistake in following

Revelation and, in consequence, in following tradition. There is something infallible in the natural instinct of animals, and also in the 'supernatural instinct' of men; but man is the only 'animal' capable of going against nature as such, either wrongly by violating it, or else by transcending it.

3

Is there a Natural
Mysticism?

The concept of a 'natural mysticism'[1] is a *petitio principii* which
enables one to assign to a class, as if once and for all, forms of
spirituality not entering into the framework of a given religion,
which is held to be the sole true and supernatural religion: it is
then maintained that even a spirituality which may seem to be
on the highest level, but which is situated outside this framework, remains in fact enclosed within the created; it may
perhaps attain the centre or the summit of this, but could not in
any way transcend it, since man can do nothing without God
and since, so it is argued, God intervenes directly only in the
one supernatural religion that exists, and not outside it. It will
readily be admitted that supernatural graces could be bestowed
on some non-christian[2] saint, but these graces will be held to
have an 'irregular', seemingly accidental character, and to be
produced not by virtue of this saint's religion, but despite it.

The principal objection to this view is that the 'created' is not
absolutely—nor in every respect—'created', or in other words
that there cannot be an absolute relativity,[3] otherwise the
created would not be distinct from nothingness, which amounts

[1] Or 'natural religion', which amounts broadly speaking to the same
thing. The term 'natural mysticism' is used here and throughout the
chapter to translate 'mystique naturelle' despite the equivocal meaning
of the word 'mysticism' in English. Here 'mysticism' always denotes
'understanding of the Mysteries' or what relates to a supra-rational
communication with Divinity. (German, *Mystik*, not *Mysticismus*.)
(Translator's note.)

[2] This concept of 'natural mysticism' in fact saw the light of day in
the Christian world, although, logically, it could serve the cause of no
matter what dogmatism.

[3] There can be a relative absoluteness, as we have explained elsewhere, and this asymmetry shows, precisely, that the absolute and the
real coincide. The possibility of relative reality does not entail that of
an absolutely real relativity, or in other words the absolute reality of
relativity as such.

to saying, in ordinary language, that it would be nonexistent; the 'uncreated' or the 'supernatural' then lies concealed in the 'created', the 'natural', and can be attained, in principle, by the Intellect which, indeed, comprises in its essence a 'supernatural' or 'uncreated' element. If the supernatural is in things by virtue of their very Existence, it is by the Intellect that it can be actualised, so that the two supernatural poles of the created are pure Existence and pure Intellect; the supernatural is essentially 'Being' and 'Intelligence', or 'Reality' and 'Consciousness'. But the antimetaphysical and purely 'phenomenalist' character of the thesis of 'natural mysticism' appears above all in the denial of the metaphysical transparency of things, or in the prejudice which considers creatures only in respect of their separative 'projection'.

It is important to state here that the supernatural or the divine is quite evidently not 'contained' in the created or the world, despite certain appearances, but that it is in principle accessible starting from its traces in the cosmos, which is quite different; in other words, things—thanks to their Existence—and the intellective subject—thanks to Knowledge—open concrete ways towards the Absolute. There is no question here either of 'pantheism' or of 'panentheism', for we are saying, not that the world as such is God or that it contains God, but simply that the world, in so far as it exists—or that it is not nonexistent—is an aspect of its divine Cause, hence 'something of God'; the Divinity, while being absolutely transcendent in relation to the world, is none the less 'present' at the centre of all cosmic reality. The world shows its 'divine quality' in two ways: firstly by the miracle of its Existence, as we have just said, and secondly—on the basis or within the framework of that miracle—by its multiple and inexhaustible symbolism which manifests the Infinite in the most diversified ways. Equally, the Intellect 'is divine', first because it is a knower—or because it is not a non-knower—and secondly because it reduces all phenomena to their Principle; because it sees the Cause in every effect, and thus surmounts, at a certain level, the vertiginous and devouring multiplicity of the phenomenal world. When we say that the Intellect 'is not a non-knower', or that the world 'is not non-existent', we are expressing a shade of meaning which is far from insignificant, for the negative expression here emphasises, more strongly than does the positive, the necessary and self-evident character of the enunciation.

Existence crystallises, divides and disperses; Intelligence, on the contrary, brings back to unity; however, if subjects— human, animal, angelic or others—are multiple, it is precisely because they are in Existence and because, by this fact, the principle of Existence diversifies them; inversely, if universal Existence is one, this is because it proceeds from the divine Intellect, manifesting it in crystallising mode without thereby losing its metaphysical homogeneity. Once a thing exists, there is in it 'all that exists', hence Existence or, indeed, absolute Reality, of which Existence is only the 'illusory dimension' advancing towards 'nothingness'; equally, there is in every act of knowledge 'all that knows', hence the Principle of all possible knowledge, namely the divine Subject or the Self; but this Subject is in itself beyond the polarisation into subject and object.

In order to avoid all misunderstanding, it must be emphasised that this involves no question of any kind of naturalism; we are not saying either that the Intellect suffices in fact for salvation, or that it can be wholly effective in the absence of a traditional wisdom; what must be said is that the Intellect, once it is in fact 'deployed' in virtue of a pre-existing wisdom, suffices for knowing wherein salvation consists and what will be its conditions; the Intellect once actualised carries its criteria within itself. The 'subjective supernatural' has need— 'accidentally' and not 'essentially'—of the 'objective supernatural', but once it is thus 'awakened to itself' by what corresponds to it outside of us, no extrinsic objection can concern it further. It is sometimes said that no proof exists of the validity of the Intellect; this is a contradiction in terms, for the fact that such a proof cannot be furnished to meet a particular artificial need of causality, or that possible proofs are inaccessible to such and such an intelligence, in no way invalidates the self-evidence of truth, any more than the eventual impossibility of proving to the mad that we are sane and they are not removes anything from the objective fact of our sanity or the consciousness that we have of it; and if, according to an argument as facile as it is absurd, everything in the intelligence, even mathematical evidence, can be illusion, the same hypothesis can also be applied, *a fortiori*, to the external or objective proofs of a conviction. If everything in pure intelligence could be delusion, everything in phenomena could also be so, with still less improbability, for phenomena are made for intelligence and not the reverse; miracles are not done for animals. But in reality both hypotheses are absurd, since both intelligence and intelligibility exist; if there is intelligence, there must be something intelligible, and if there is something to understand, there must be a mind to understand it. There can be false phenomena, false miracles for example, but there cannot be evidence at once false and intellectual, whether it be a question of mathematics or of metaphysics; an oasis can be a mirage, but 2 and 2 cannot not make 4, nor can the world be deprived of a transcendent cause. To claim, for the sake of furthering some argument or other, that one of the poles—intellectual or existential—of the Universe is illusory on its own plane—for all is illusory in relation to the eternal actuality of God—annuls at the same time the respective complementary pole and ends logically in complete nihilism.

However that may be, we have to distinguish between one perspective which is intellectual and unitive, and another which is existential and separative: the first envisages everything in relation to unity, even Existence ('all is *Atmâ*'), while the second sees everything in relation to separativity, even Intelligence ('the intellect does not reach beyond the created', etc.); this second perspective is, in fact, 'cosmo-centric' and 'phenomenalist', not theocentric and metaphysical. According to this second view, the world is comparable to concentric circles which, while reflecting the centre, never attain it, so that there is absolute separation; according to the first perspective, on the contrary, the world is like a star, every ray of which unites the periphery to the central point; and this perspective, which is that of 'metaphysical transparency' or 'essential identity', sees God in everything that exists, and 'sees' Him or 'realises' Him in a certain manner in the impersonal and universal mystery of the Intellect. Now it is a matter of combining these two modes of vision, for each is valid in its own way; it is certain that things—as such—are infinitely separated from the Principle and that consequently there is no continuity possible between It and them, but it is also just as true, in another respect, that things—by virtue of their essential reality, that is to say of their pure existence and their immediate symbolism—'are not other than the Principle', if one can so express it, failing which they would be either a second Absolute, or a nothingness pure and simple. If we combine the image of the concentric circles with that of the star, we obtain the spider's web, which is a particularly intelligible symbol of the cosmos; the concentric circles could also be replaced by the spiral which, ending as it does in the centre, thus marks the 'divine continuity' of the cosmos; or again, the centre of the star could be removed so as to have rays converging on a luminous void, thus marking the infinity of the divine Centre.

With all these images, which despite their apparent simplicity verge upon the limit of what is humanly expressible, we wish to convey the idea that the 'supernatural' resides above all in the nature of things and not, essentially and exclusively, in some condition belonging to the phenomenal order—as it were a *deus ex machina*. Such conditions can certainly attach themselves to the existential and intellective supernatural, and thus allow spiritual virtuality to become actualised, but their relatively circumstantial function excludes, precisely, the possibility of a complete monopoly of the supernatural; in other words, if the supernatural already resides in the metaphysical structure of the created, without for all that being reducible to the 'natural', this implies that it has a character of universality and that, therefore, it cannot not offer itself to man, in one form or another, wherever it meets with the necessary receptivity; and this receptivity with regard to the supernatural is proved by the existence of a corresponding wisdom where in most cases prejudice is willing to see only 'natural mysticism'. It is true that an apparently rational and practically anthropocentric aspect of the Shankarian *Vedanta* or of the Buddhist *Dhamma* is liable to convey the impression of a purely human wisdom, but this is simply a matter of external dialectic and technical opportuneness, and not of mental limitation; this is proved on the one hand by the transcendent character of these doctrines, which becomes evident when they are envisaged in their totality, and on the other hand by the fact that they are always accompanied by initiations, which are by definition super-natural, since it is this characteristic that constitutes their reason for existing; from another angle, spiritual currents such as those connected with Vishnu and Amida Buddha are ways of grace or of mercy and have not, as such, any rationalising aspect, at least no more than is found in Christianity.

Some will perhaps consider that the term 'natural mysticism' is nevertheless not devoid of meaning; it is not in fact possible that a mysticism lying entirely on the human level should not occur somewhere, since confusions lie within the possibilities of man as such; but then it will be a false mysticism, so that the term 'natural mysticism' constitutes either an error or an abuse of language; a 'mysticism' is false which is ignorant of the supernatural, either through denying it, or by wrongly claiming it for itself, since such a mysticism is evidently cut off from all 'mystery'. The sacred and age-old traditions of the East are there to show that such cannot be the case for a wisdom which, being a receptacle of divine life, cannot lack the corresponding content, and that, in this realm more than in any other, the Spirit 'bloweth where it listeth'.

The great contradiction between the postulate of a 'natural mysticism' and its complement, the Judaeo-Christian conception of the 'supernatural', is thus seen to result from the fact that the terms of this distinction are applied contrary to the nature of things: in the one case a given wisdom is labelled 'natural' although it transcends essentially all that is 'nature', whilst in the other case certain given factors are brought into the 'supernatural', although they in no way belong outside the realm of phenomena. It even seems as if the wisdom of such and such a 'foreign' religion were being blamed because it was not similarly limited, or, rather, the fact that it is not so limited is explained away in terms of a deceptive lack of realism, even a lack of sincerity; speculations which have been developed to the limit of the expressible are qualified as 'dreams in the abstract', as if such an appreciation were not, to say the least, a confession of metaphysical incompetence. There is always the same reversal of normal relationships: the 'phenomenal' element in practice plays the part of a *deus ex machina* to the detriment of such and such a principial, and therefore supra-phenomenal truth, and of such and such an effective knowledge of the same order; a question-begging formula is substituted for what is evident and thereby also for the imprescriptible rights of what constitutes our very Essence. But since a verbal fiction does not suffice to change the nature of things, the falseness of the postulate in question is fatally betrayed by the 'gaps' in a logic which aims at being impeccable and disinterested, but uses processes of 'objective analysis' which are illusions at least as pernicious as those that one expects to uncover in a hypothetical 'natural mysticism'.

The differences between traditional forms translate what constitutes the sufficient reason of each; but for those who seek to resolve every difficulty by the hypothesis of a 'natural' mysticism or religion, these differences can only indicate so many deviations from the one unique religion, or so many different ways of placing oneself outside the only 'supernatural' recognised as valid. Without asking oneself, for example, what impression the 'Song of Songs'[1] might make on a Buddhist monk, the Mahâyâna *sutras* are taken for poetic artifices, as if there could be effects without a cause; that is to say, as if the spiritual and moral force of the 'Great Vehicle', its extraordinary vitality and the profundity of its art, could be explained as arising from fantasies of the imagination—or as if the immensity of the result in space and time, affecting societies, cultures and souls, did not reflect the greatness and the quality of absoluteness in the prime mover. When these Scriptures are criticised for their legendary character while the strictly historical nature of the Gospels is emphasised, a most important criterion is forgotten, namely the efficacy of the sacred text; if this efficacy is in fact guaranteed, for a naturally contemplative and symbolist mentality, by a more or less mythological form, of what use is an historicity which this mentality does not require?[2]

Another example of the 'optical illusion' in question is the following: some people consider that the ineluctability of the law of *karma* annuls, logically, *Amitabha's* power of mercy; but predestination, which no theologian can deny in full awareness, unless he also denies that God 'knew' the destiny of every creature even 'before' the creation—predestination, we say, is opposed just as much—or just as little—to the redeeming power of Christ. Or again: it is recognised that in Buddhism *Nirvana* comes before the Buddha, so that the latter is, as it were, an expression of the former—an expression which, as such, is 'illusory'—whilst in the Judaeo-Christian perspective it is on the contrary God who comes before Paradise, that is to say

---

[1] Is this 'oriental poem', that St. Bernard and others have taken the trouble to commentate, less strange in its literalness than the *Sukhâvati-Vyûhas*, leaving aside any question of taste?

[2] In the same line of ideas, it may be noted that it is in the nature of esotericism to base itself externally on some precarious and often almost imperceptible element, to announce itself as it were casually, and this explains how it is that the last sermons of the Buddha—the authenticity of which is sometimes questioned—were unfolded as it were 'on the fringe of' the more exoteric teaching. The New Testament basis for Hesychasm—to add this one example—has the same character of precariousness.

Paradise is in a certain way reducible to God; this latter point of view could evidently be regarded as the more 'supernatural',[1] but the refusal to admit or to understand the former—once one has studied it—has basically a very 'natural' explanation, namely the anti-metaphysical horror of 'nothingness' and the desire never to lose contact with the human[2]—the desire to instal the human and the individual even in the Divine, and also to situate the Absolute in a sublimated human. The absoluteness of man and of history entails the humanity and historicity of the Absolute, and inversely.

Again, an argument that is far from being negligible is that of miracles: why does God allow miracles if not in order to say something? We are not thinking here, of course, of the prodigies with which legend loves to adorn the memory of saints, but of the signs, supernatural—because they have a divine cause, although they appear evidently in nature—by which God favours His elect, or some amongst them; an apparently miraculous fact proves nothing in itself, certainly, but it proves everything when it can be placed positively in connection with a traditional spirituality and is accompanied by criteria which guarantee its authenticity. Whatever may be the gulf that

[1] Needless to say we have no 'preference' for one or the other, since each is legitimate from its own point of view and they are qualitatively equivalent.

[2] An 'optical illusion' of this kind appears in a certain type of Hindu *bhakti* that is ready to postulate a supreme spiritual experience placed beyond all, even supra-formal, knowledge, which amounts to saying that there could be an experience which would in no sense be knowledge. Correspondingly, this same 'mytho-theology' speaks of a divine personal 'form' manifesting beyond the supra-formal divine Reality, which proves simply that such a perspective confuses the supra-formal, which eminently embraces all 'form', with the amorphous, or that it confuses the non-differentiated Consciousness (*prajna*) of the Self with the 'dark night' of 'extinction'. The very human desire to be thus at the summit seems rather characteristic of the perspectives of love, although it accords ill with their climate of 'humility'; the same reproach does not arise, however, in relation to the sapiential perspectives, for the hierarchy of values exists; it is independent of our desires and our choices.

separates one religious language from another, these signs are often the same: thus, the contemporaries of Honen Shonin, the most illustrious representative of Japanese Amidism, observed in their master the same phenomena of luminosity and of reading at night without either lamp or candle as the contemporaries of the great St. Teresa were to observe some centuries later; or again, this same Honen had visions, shared sometimes by those around him, of Buddhas and Bodhisattvas, just as our mystics of the West have been able to behold Christ and the Virgin: in each case there is the same clarity of vision and the same effusion of graces. It would be idle to enumerate all the miraculous facts—healings, phenomena of levitation, of bilocation, and so on—by which God, whatever may be the metaphysical conception with which He is clothed in some particular Revelation, corroborates both His truth and the sanctity which flows from it, with the manifest effect of confirming the faithful in their faith; what we would underline here is quite simply that the similarities and the number of miracles in all the different religions are too great not to have significance; to assert that miracles are true on one side and false on the other is to reduce the human condition to absurdity.

4

Vicissitudes of Different
Spiritual Temperaments

Human nature is so made that it tends to enclose itself in some limitation, and this tendency can only be accentuated in an age which is everywhere engaged in destroying the framework of universality. Starting from the distinction between 'love' and 'knowledge'—or *bhakti* and *jnâna*—it may be said that the *bhakta*, the volitional and affective mind, the perspective of which is based mainly on the alternative 'charity' versus 'egoism', runs the risk of neglecting 'objective truth', while the *jnâni*, the intellective mind, which on the contrary sees things in terms of the alternative 'truth' versus 'error', is exposed to the temptation of neglecting the strictly human perfections, and perhaps even the human link with God. We are thinking here principally of 'spiritual types' and not of their corresponding realisations, above all as regards the *jnâni* who, indeed, may be somewhat lacking in 'charity' in so far as he is an 'intellectual genius'—or as he is in practice led to shut himself up in theory even while of necessity recognising its limitations—but not in so far as he is a 'realised' or 'delivered spirit'[1]; on the other hand *bhakti*, which comprises more 'elementary' and 'easier' realisations—because of necessity they do not go beyond the human plane—is conceivable apart from intellectuality properly so called, and even, although doubtless only in a partial way, outside the bounds of strict orthodoxy. A bhaktic perfection from which the 'intellectual' element is lacking—in one form or another—is like a body without a skeleton, since it is situated outside its normal and necessary surroundings, namely a traditional civilisation; this latter precisely performs

[1] Strictly speaking, it is only in the latter case that the term *jnâni* is applicable. The word 'intellectual' is used here as elsewhere by us strictly as referring to the Intellect, it does not apply to the purely 'mental' speculations of logicians.

the function of an 'external skeleton' for the *bhakta*: it is the
tradition which 'thinks' for him and neutralises the more or less
inevitable 'extravagances' of the bhaktic devotee. We can
sacrifice our judgment, as obedience sometimes demands, but
only on condition of being certain that this judgement is still
exercised around us in the traditional environment. In an
inversely analogous way, a jnanic perfection from which
the element 'charity' is lacking or which some concession to
mental passion deprives of the serenity connatural with
contemplation, is like a skeleton without flesh: here it is beauty
of the soul which provides the normal 'environment' or
'climate', or which is the complement, not of intellection as
such, but of the mental activity resulting from it; this beauty has
its source in peace and generosity—but not in any vagueness or
woolliness—and is inherent in *jnâna* so far as this can be
identified with pure gnosis.

One sees from this confrontation that the condition of
equilibrium or of integrality is 'external' at the same time as
indirectly 'intellectual' with the volitional man, and 'internal'
at the same time as apparently 'moral' with the intellectual
man; we say 'indirectly' because the traditional surroundings
assert themselves above all through symbolism, and 'apparently'
because the charity of the *jnâni* is not so much an individual or
psychological attitude as an impersonal conformity to what
'pre-exists' *in divinis*. *Bhakti* is still situated, *a priori* and as a
Way, on the human plane, while *jnâna*—or the Intellect which
is at the same time both its 'seat' and its 'organ'—lies beyond
the *ego*; the distinctive 'quality' of the *jnâni* is thus not strictly
speaking human, for it does not properly belong to any individual: it is the Spirit that 'bloweth where it listeth' and of
which one cannot tell 'whence it cometh, nor whither it goeth'.[1]

[1] As Coomaraswamy has pointed out with truly Hindu boldness,
'there always remains a last step, in which ritual is abandoned and the
relative truths of theology are denied. As it was by the knowledge of
good and evil that man fell from his first estate, so it must be
from the knowledge of good and evil, from the moral law, that he must
be delivered at last. However far one may have gone, there remains a

Nevertheless, for the jnanic contemplative there must be something that performs the function of an external and symbolist framework, just as for the *bhakta* there must be something that corresponds to the 'inner environment' of the *jnâni*: this external framework of the *jnâni* will be beauty, in its aspect of intelligibility, of symbolism 'lived' or of harmony, and not in its aspect of superficial charm; it is this which, without being actually indispensable, none the less constitutes the natural and providential complement of intellective concentration—itself 'abstract' in a certain relative sense—and hence an indirect element of equilibrium; it is like a perfume of truth allowing the intelligence to come to rest without suspicion. Moreover, it is not without reason that the beauty in question should be the beauty of virgin nature rather than of temples: for

last step to be taken, involving a dissolution of all former values. A church or society—the Hindu would make no distinction—that does not provide a way of escape from its own regimen, and will not let its people go, is defeating its own ultimate purpose'. (*Hinduism and Buddhism*, Part I, 'The Social Order'.)—It is not a question here exclusively of *jnâna*, but of a reality which is in any case nearer to *jnâna* than to *bhakti*. It may be added that the freedom of being outside forms can be quite interior, and is of necessity so, to a greater or less degree, in the religions of Semitic origin, where spirituality takes a social form and where, consequently, the part is indissolubly connected with the whole; but even here, there are cases of passing beyond all form: Mary Magdalene, the anchorite Paul, Mary of Egypt and others lived without sacraments during long years, when they were already saints. All the same, since it is necessary to pass outside forms 'upwards' and not 'downwards', the principle in question could not furnish the least excuse for complacency, or for an arbitrary and individualistic rejection of dogmas and rites.—Hermits and wandering pilgrims constitute an essential aspect of the Church—of every Church —and their disappearance, in no matter what civilisation, is a calamity having incalculable effects; contrary to popular prejudice, nothing is less 'useless' to society than the compensatory and purifying presence of those who are 'dead in this life'. Whether one likes it or not, there are spiritual modes which do not admit of being 'brigaded' any more than the wind which 'bloweth where it listeth'. Even if man can, in principle, 'die to himself' under any circumstances and so also in the world, this by no means implies that he can always do so in fact, nor that the vocations of silence and solitude do not preserve all their rights, without which the monastic life itself could not be justified.

nature reflects something of the spontaneous and the unlimited, something also of the timeless closely corresponding with the quite primordial freedom of pure Intellect; the spirit of the *jnâni* is indeed 'anterior' to all crystallisation, it is everywhere and nowhere.[1] As for *bhakti*, the 'inner environment' which it demands is none other than intelligence—not such as constitutes the qualification for gnosis, of course, but discernment on the phenomenal and rational plane; one is reminded that St. Teresa of Avila never admitted that nuns need be stupid. What matters in the first place for the *bhakta* is perfection of will and not of intelligence; hence his tendency to underestimate the latter, as if perfection of will could dispense with the truth which determines the direction and modes of that will.

All these considerations can be summed up as follows: if we see in *jnâna* a 'virile' way and in *bhakti* a 'feminine' way,[2] we would say that this virility requires an extrinsic feminine complement, or even a double complement, the one 'internal' and moral and the other 'external' and aesthetic, and that bhaktic femininity requires in its turn a double virile complement, the one external and traditional and the other internal and mental; in other words, love has need of a complement of intelligence or discernment, in its traditional surroundings and eventually also in the soul, according to the stage it has attained on the way, whilst intellectual activity has need of a complement of beauty, in the soul and secondarily in the visible environment. It is necessary to avoid mental disquiet, its unconscious

[1] It is sometimes said that the ancient hermits, notably the Desert Fathers, used to seek out the most 'desolate' places in nature, and this is thought to provide an argument against an 'aestheticism' which is anyway quite irrelevant; it is forgotten that these 'desolate' spots are neither factory walls nor office furnishings and that it is actually impossible for them to lie outside the span of beauty, for the simple reason that in virgin nature beauty is everywhere, both in severity and in softness. The nonformal must never be confused with the shapeless, nor above all with the trivial.

[2] By contrast, *bhakti* comprises, on the plane of the will, an aspect of virility or resolution, and *jnâna*, on the plane of the Intellect, an aspect of femininity or receptivity.

'egoism' and its sclerosis, as well as an opaque sentimentalism which believes that by some virtue or other it can make up for absence of truth.

Before going further, it is perhaps desirable to state, once again, that intellectual genius must not be confused with the mental acuteness of logicians: intellectual intuition comprises essentially a contemplativity which in no way enters into the rational capacity, the latter being logical rather than contemplative; it is contemplative power, receptivity in respect of the Uncreated Light, the opening of the Eye of the Heart, which distinguishes transcendent intelligence from reason. The latter perceives the general and proceeds by logical operations, whilst Intellect perceives the principial—the metaphysical—and proceeds by intuition. Intellection is concrete in relation to rational abstractions, and abstract in relation to the divine Concrete; from another point of view we should be tempted to say that logic is to intellectual intuition as the latter is to effective gnosis, although the terms in question are not strictly comparable. 'Genius' is not in the Intellect as such, but in the receptacle: it is a 'supernaturally natural' cleft in human opacity.

Now, one might ask oneself why the soul of the intellective is required to make an effort of charity, at any rate—or above all—in conditions so abnormal as to deprive it of a traditional moral culture, while at the same time obliging it to put the emphasis on theory; to this we would reply that the relationship between knowledge and virtue, which evidently is indirect, signifies, not that Intellect is insufficient and has need of extrinsic help, but that man is not the Intellect and that absence of virtue can lead, in one degree or another, to a split between man and his intelligence: man can be the infallible mouthpiece of the Spirit, but the relationship between the one and the other is a grace, except where the 'Self' has absorbed the 'I' to the point of leaving nothing but a transparent screen. Apart from this sublime station, it avails a man nothing to be infallible on some particular plane, his infallibility provides no security pact between him and God; his intelligence can be darkened, or rather, it can withdraw, and then it is the man and not intelligence that is darkened; the mind can wear itself out when the soul neglects to 'repose in God', but Intellect remains intact. Metaphysics is beyond charity, it is true, but a metaphysician without charity seriously risks compromising the doctrine because of the indirect repercussions of his vice on the workings of his intelligence. According to a very wise remark of St. Theresa of the Child-Jesus—a remark we have had occasion to quote elsewhere—St. Peter would not have denied Christ if, instead of relying on his own strength in asserting that he would never deny him, he had added: 'with thy help', and so: 'with God's help'. In fact, the danger for the intelligence, whether it be ordinary or superior (though in the latter case it is its 'non-divine face' alone that is in question) is to place too much trust not in its light as such, which is normal, but in the presence of that light; this presence depends on grace, as we have said, for no man has the power to create his own spirit. However that may be, it is important to know how to combine contradictory truths: we mean that the Intellect possesses not only the aspect of a 'gift', but also that of a 'personal essence'; this latter aspect neutralises the former, in proportion to the power or the 'actualisation' of the intellective grace. In short, if man can 'have' the Truth, he can also 'be' it.

An objection might here be raised that charity requires to be transcended in gnosis and that it is illogical to concern oneself with it since Knowledge, being beyond oppositions, contains the undifferentiated quintessence of every virtue; to this the reply must be made that positive charity is necessary in so far as the individual has not understood the meaning of negative virtue; the *jnâni* asks, not: 'Am I charitable?' but: 'Is this being free of egoism?', that is to say his virtue is as negative as his theosophy[1]

---

[1] Theosophy in the proper sense of the word, of course, and not some form of neo-spiritualism. Theosophy, which is none other than doctrinal gnosis, is distinguished from theology by the fact that in essence it is wisdom and has no call to concern itself with the question of what is opportune.

is apophatic. Intrinsic virtue lies beyond all moral specification; it is our fundamental being, so that to be virtuous means to abstain from the vices of fallen nature. This by no means prevents abstention from being able to assume, according to circumstances, an aspect of volitive affirmation, hence of exteriorisation and activity. On the other hand the strictly moral perspective, which the *jnâni* or the 'gnostic' has to leave behind, implies adding works and virtues to our being and thereby tends toward individualism; in practice it runs the risk of putting works and virtues in the place of God, while the jnanic perspective, which confines itself to maintaining the soul in the virginity of our fundamental being, is impersonal from the fact that it sees virtue, not in human initiatives, but in an existential quality, namely the primordial and innocent nature of the created; but this fundamental being, or this theomorphic nature, is an ontological level deeper than the level of the fall. Virtue is then not dissociated from contemplation, it rests, so to speak, in God; it is less a will to do than a consciousness of being, and that is why it withdraws from the plane of moral oppositions instead of entering actively into their play. But the transcending of the virtues could not in any case be equivalent to an absence of virtues; on the contrary, it means freedom from the individual limitations which the divine Qualities assume in the human ego[1]; what counts most, for God, is the quality of our

---

[1] The irreversible relationship between 'good' and 'being'—the first state being reducible to the second and there finding its essence, but the second being independent and transcendent in relation to the first—this relationship is expressed by the term *sattwa*, which designates the ascending cosmic tendency, and so also 'good' as such, referring as it does etymologically to *Sat*, 'Being'.—'He only *is* free from virtues and vices and all their fatal consequences, who has never become anyone; he only *can* be free who is no longer anyone; impossible to be freed from oneself and also to remain oneself. The liberation from good and evil that seemed impossible and is indeed impossible for man whom we define by what he does or thinks, one who answers the question "Who is that?", "It's me", is possible only for him who can answer at the Sun-door to the question "Who art thou?", "Thyself".' (Ananda K. Coomaraswamy, *Hinduism and Buddhism*, Part 1, ch. 'Theology and Autology'.)

contemplation, for to be contemplated is for God a manner of 'being', if one may so express it, in the sense that the fact of human contemplation is a consequence of divine 'being'.

*

The *bhakta* distinguishes *a priori* between God and the *ego*, between 'other' and 'I'. The 'other' in practice functions as God in the sense of the familiar Gospel teaching[1]; but the *ego* will denote for the *bhakta*—and more especially in neo-bhaktism—the quintessence of all evil, to the extent of replacing the devil, as if the latter had ceased to exist outside us; the dangers of such a simplification are counterbalanced, it is true, by the traditional quality of the environment, but this safeguard ceases to operate as soon as those surroundings are quitted. To reduce the devil to the *ego* amounts in practice to abolishing him, and in consequence to forgetting the powers of illusion; the door then stands open to a puerile optimism, which is all the more dangerous in that it is mingled unsuspectingly with optimism about 'progress' and readily accepts the tendency of the modern world to belittle and falsify everything. Further-more an over-exclusive—and indeed inconsequent—'satanisa-tion' of the *ego* entails an over-simplicist 'divinisation' of the 'other'; that is to say that the replacing of the devil by the 'I' goes hand in hand with replacing God by the 'neighbour', whence an 'altruism' which appears as an end in itself and thus loses all contact with metaphysical truth, and so with genuine

[1] In Christian language people speak of 'pride' rather than of 'ego'. Let us add that both Catholic and Orthodox *bhaktas* are protected by dogma, which is scarcely the case for the Hindu *bhakta*, who is on the one hand more 'universalist' than the Christian, but on the other more vulnerable, at least in our times. 'Narrowness' is sometimes a protection; 'breadth' is admirable only when it can be sustained. The classical *bhakti* of India was very narrow in relation to *jnâna*; it was Ramakrishna who 'broadened' it, he who was at the same time *bhakta* and *jnâni*, which in no way means that every *bhakta* must or can follow his example.

spirituality.[1] In such a perspective, the distinction, essential though it is, between truth and error is obliterated: it is the *ego* as such which alone is regarded as 'error', and God and the neighbour who alone are regarded as 'truth'; there is then nothing wrong in believing that two and two make five, provided one 'does good' or 'renders service'.

But since it is never possible to hold in a completely consistent way that error is 'I', one is forced to exclude from egoity various manifestations of the *ego*, thus adding to the latter yet one illusion the more; similarly, since it is impossible to admit without contradiction that truth is the 'other', one inevitably ends by mixing up the notions of truth and of God, which moreover quite accords with a contempt—tricked out as humility—for the intelligence. From here it is but a step to acceptance of Antichrist out of humility or charity, even out of 'good manners'. In a general way, *bhaktas* have a certain interest in depreciating the intelligence: 'intellectual pride'—or what is believed to be such—is rejected only to be replaced by an attitude of pride towards the Intellect, as if this second pride were preferable to the first, and so one slips into the sin against the Holy Ghost.

The two positions of which we have just spoken above— situating the devil in the *ego* and God in the neighbour—are all the same perfectly well founded, provided that they are kept

---

[1] 'But as regards the individuality, we shall be able to say, "Such an one no longer loves himself or others: he is the Self in himself and in them. Death to one's self is death to 'others'; and if the 'dead man' seems to be 'unselfish', this will not be the result of altruistic motive, but accidentally, and because he is literally un-self-ish. Liberated from himself, from all status, all duties, all rights, he has become a Mover-at-Will (*kâmachârî*), like the Spirit (*Vâyu, âtmâ devânâm*) that 'moveth as it will' (*yathâ vasham carati*) and as St. Paul expresses it, 'no longer under the law.'"' (Ananda K. Coomaraswamy, *Hinduism and Buddhism*, Part I, ch. 'Theology and Autology'.)—'The mere presence of these men in a society to which they no longer belong, by its affirmation of ultimate values, affects all values . . . Blessed is the man on whose tomb can be written, *Hic jacet nemo*.' (Ibid., Part I, ch. 'The Social Order'.)

within their indispensable context: they are only valid, that is to say, in a certain relationship and not in any other, or more precisely they impose themselves on the moral plane and as a remedy against our natural egoism, but not outside the polarity *ego-alter* and the problem of egoity. The intelligence which distinguishes us from animals is a gift of God by the same token as charity, and the latter is not even possible without the former; it is not enough to be 'harmless as doves', it is also necessary to be 'wise as serpents': against the exclusiveness of a moral and 'subjectivist' idealism—an exclusiveness that is impracticable in a world that is breaking down—it is needful to maintain the 'discerning of spirits' in the very interest of the idealism in question, for the latter is necessary to us from a certain point of view, but not from every point of view. There is a 'feminine' quality in moral subjectivism when it is taken in isolation and mingled with the sentimentality which is implied in ratio to its degree of artificial isolation; but complete femininity corresponds to a 'part' and not to a 'totality'[1] so that the feminising of spirituality can only mark a disequilibrium and a movement towards dissolution; it is the substituting of 'colours' for 'forms' or of 'sounds' for 'rhythms'. That femininity is a necessary element in all spirituality,[2] we would not think of contesting, but one must know how to put each thing in its place.

The question of 'altruism' calls for the insertion here of a few remarks on lay and antitraditional 'humanitarianism' which an unreflecting sentimentality too easily confuses with the

[1] The egalitarianism that has resulted, by deviation and under modern influences, from the bhaktic refusal to make distinctions that are more or less 'passional', or deemed to be such, has given rise to a 'feminism' hardly compatible with *bhakti*. Feminism, far from being able to confer on woman 'rights' that are non-existent because contrary to the nature of things, can only remove from her her specific dignity; it is the abolition of the eternal-feminine, of the glory that woman derives from her celestial prototype. After all, the revolt of one sex against the other, like the cult of youth or the contempt of intelligence, is indirectly a revolt against God.

[2] As is proved—if proof were needed—by the mystical role of the Virgin-Mother.

charity of saints. This 'humanitarianism' in fact puts itself forward as a philosophy founded on the idea that man is good; but to believe that man is good is almost always to believe that God is bad, or that He would be bad 'if He existed'; and as modern men believe less and less in God—apart from a totally inoperative scientific 'deism'—they pour out over God's representatives the resentment that they would like to show against God Himself: man is good, they think, but religions are bad; priests, who have invented religions in order to bolster up their own interests and perpetuate their privileges, are bad, and so on. It is the satanic inversion of the traditional axiom that God is good and man is bad: God can be called 'good' because all possible goodness derives from Him and every quality expresses—in an 'indirectly direct' manner—His Essence, and not only such and such a function; and man is bad because his will no longer conforms to the profound nature of things, hence to the divine 'Being', and his false 'instinct of self-preservation' makes itself the advocate of every passion and every terrestrial illusion.[1] Many men are good only 'by accident', that is to say in the absence of circumstances which might actualise in them all the baseness, ferocity and perfidy of which human nature is capable; it is true that there exists in every man a deeper layer, a 'pre-satanic' layer one might say, and this latter is good, but it finds itself buried, precisely, under the 'icy' crust produced by the 'fall' and now become second nature. Only the love of God—or gnosis—can break or melt this ice; as for a deliberately 'human' virtue, a virtue attributable solely to the resources of our corrupted nature, this is merely a defiance hurled at God; basically it tries to show that man is better than God, or that man alone is good—man 'despiritualised' and thereby 'de-humanised'. In reality, the busy activity of human kind is a

---

[1] Let us recall here that the negative aspects of God are extrinsic and derive from relativity, that is to say from the remoteness of the world from the Principle; this remoteness—or the world, which amounts to the same thing—derives in its turn from the divine Infinity, which calls for the 'illusorily real' possibility of its own negation. We are here approaching the verge of the inexpressible.

very small thing: man can neither create good nor destroy evil; in the long run he can but change a little the pattern of evil or good; and when he does so in the name of an atheistic and demagogic prometheanism, he ends only in destroying values higher than those he is capable of envisaging, and in engendering evils greater than those that he set out to overcome.[1] Ordinary man is no doubt capable of providing for his needs and avoiding certain calamities, but the saint alone burns up the very roots of evil, not in the whole world doubtless, 'for it must needs be that offences come', but in particular surroundings and according to the economy of Providence.

It would certainly be absurd to assert that human beings are fundamentally bad; but with the best will in the world one cannot find in man the innocence of virgin nature. As Moses sang, man is 'like grass which groweth up . . . in the evening it is cut down and withereth', which would be in no way abnormal if man were merely grass; but precisely we are beings much too conscious to be 'fully entitled' to be as miserable as in fact we are. If man is good, why seek to protect him against himself —for what enemy has he outside his own species—and if religion is a human thing (given there is no God), how is it reasonable to reproach it with having dragged man down? And if human evil has a source outside man, whence does it come? Not from animality, for the animal, however savage, is in-

---

[1] How self-defeating are the aims of humanitarianism is to be observed in the fact that it readily accepts what is most inhuman, namely the cult of machinery, which suppresses artisanship and thereby one of the conditions of human happiness; there was much merit in Gandhi's campaign against the machine, and consequently on behalf of human dignity. Humanitarianism pretends to seek the good of man, but it is blind to things which, from the spiritual and even simply human point of view, deserve to be called 'atrocities', such as the trivialities of advertisements and so forth which infest modern life causing damage in quite another way than did the epidemics of ancient times; for triviality surrounds us everywhere, bringing dirt and death to souls. Before laying down the law as to man's needs and the remedies they require, it is necessary to know what man is; it is necessary to envisage the human being in his totality, or not be concerned with him at all.

capable of human perversion. The fact of which antitraditional humanitarianism has completely lost sight is that evils on earth are inevitable because the world is not God, or because the effect is not the Cause; the discrepancy between the two terms must be manifested in the term which is relative, and that is precisely the meaning of suffering and death. Man escapes this fatality only in the Absolute. We do not say that he cannot avoid certain evils on a limited plane, but we do say that he cannot avoid evil as such, which is quite a different thing. The attitude of convinced optimists is, in practice, to choose the world whilst wishing that it were not the world. 'Seek ye first the kingdom of God, and his righteousness; and all these things shall be added unto you', says the Gospel.

This digression allows us to assess more easily the danger that modern influences involve for non-doctrinal and 'practical' *bhakti*; in the case of certain Hindu 'reformers' we have seen how a profane humanitarianism, which they evidently did not recognise as such, overflowed nevertheless into their 'theology'; in order to save God's honour, or to excuse His existence, it was necessary to reduce God to the collective soul, thus leaving Him some place in an ill-defined subjective experience. In a general way, one thing that Orientals who seek to be spiritual as well as westernised seem not to understand is that, if their fathers had thought 'freely' like themselves as little as two centuries ago, there would today be no spirituality, either 'conservative' or, still less, 'progressive'; in other words these spiritual persons live on a heritage that they despise and are squandering without noticing it, just as Westerners have been doing for a long time. Modernist influence is everywhere destroying the doctrinal foundations and introducing all kinds of errors and prejudices; the result is a great deal of confusion and above all a curious lack of any sense of proportion.[1] Let us note, in this order of

[1] It happens frequently that anglicised Hindus, as also other Asiatics, mention in the same breath names like Jesus and Gandhi, Shankara and Kierkegaard, Buddha and Goethe, the Holy Virgin and Mrs. X, or affirm that such and such a German musician was a *yogi* or that the French Revolution was a mystical movement, etc. This

fact reveals a total ignorance of certain differences of category which
are none the less of capital importance—we would readily say differences of 'reality'—as well as a strange lack of sensibility; it also shows a
tendency to simplification, due doubtless to the more or less unconscious idea that only 'realisation' counts and not 'theory', whence a
completely misplaced and profitless contempt for the objective
discerning of phenomena. Is it then really necessary to remind people
that a 'great incarnation', who conforms to cyclic laws and in whom
the Deity is manifested in a 'direct' and 'active' way, differs totally,
not only from ordinary men, 'geniuses' included, but even from a
'lesser incarnation', such as takes place through a human receptacle
where the divine manifestation is in a sense 'indirect' and 'passive'?
Hinduism nevertheless distinguishes with complete clarity between
these two kinds of *Avatâras*, not to mention other subdivisions which
need not concern us here: it is plain how much forgetfulness can result
from a contempt of orthodoxy. Apart from this distinction, it is even
more clearly necessary not to confuse the sacred and the profane, nor
above all the traditional and the anti-traditional: it is inexcusable to
confuse a 'thinker' who is a stranger to all tradition, in other words
quite profane, not only with a saint—who derives by definition from
tradition and the sacred—but even with a traditional authority;
'genius' is quite independent of this question, for the least that can be
said about it is that an 'error of genius' has no value at all in regard
to the truth. A typical example of neo-Hindu deviation is the Swami
Yogananda, founder in the United States of a 'Self-Realisation
Fellowship' (SRF!), the president (!) of which is—or was—an Ameri-
can woman. On the other hand we find the 'discerning of spirits'
present to an eminent degree in a man like Coomaraswamy, and we
are not alone in hoping that his influence will grow in his own country:
'While on one side the limited range and settled canons of official
orientalism in the West and textual scholarship in India could not
often see eye to eye with him, forgetting the fact that frequently the
insight of an attuned imagination pierced to the truth more unerringly
than the eye of mere scholarship or the spectacles of philological
indexes, his expositions of the traditional view of life ran, on the other,
counter to prevalent political and social doctrines in the West . . .
which he denounced . . . as a "mechanism" in which the "whole man"
was reduced to mere "hands", "cogs in a wheel", "copies of copies"
. . . While we in India are being swept by these ideologies from the
modern West and would cry down any call to preserve tradition as
atavism, a steadily growing community of savants in the West has come
to believe in the wisdom of the teachings of Coomaraswamy . . . The
earlier we garner up the remnants of our traditional culture, the
greater the prospect of the ark of the new and free India saving itself
from deluge.' (Dr. V. Raghavan, in *Homage to Ananda Coomaraswamy*.)
—'Let no man presume to invoke the name of Coomaraswamy who,

ideas, the extreme liberty that is taken with the doctrine of the *kali-yuga* and the *Kalki-Avatâra*—of the 'dark age' and the 'universal Messiah'—a doctrine the importance of which is such that no Revelation can ignore it, whatever symbolism may happen to be used; this amounts to saying that it constitutes a criterion of orthodoxy and, thereby, of spiritual purity and wholeness. Since this truth, which is Christian as well as Hindu, being indeed found everywhere, excludes evolutionism, it is a bulwark of tradition against a most pernicious error; thus its rejection—conscious or unconscious—opens the door to every kind of betrayal and corruption. We do not deny that evolution exists within certain limits, as is indeed evident enough, but we do deny that it is a universal principle, and hence a law which affects and determines all things, including the immutable; evolution and degeneration can moreover go hand in hand, each then occurring on a different plane. However that may be, what has to be categorically rejected is the idea that truth evolves, or that revealed doctrines are the product of an evolution.

*

If true *jnâna* 'is' orthodoxy by definition, *bhakti*, for its part, 'has need' of orthodoxy—not perhaps in the case of such or such a *bhakta* taken in isolation and enjoying an inspired and supra-formal grace, but in itself and in relation to collective life, to traditional continuity. *Bhakti* cannot be a kind of 'art for art's sake', that is to say a self-sufficing experience, claiming to be an end in itself; it is true no doubt that 'all is love', but this does not mean that 'love is all', that is to say 'no matter what'; to strip love of its metaphysical substance and of its majesty is to risk depriving it of all truth and efficacy; it is to destroy with

when about to buy something new or to replace something old, forgets the local craftsman and goes and gets a factory-made article just because this happens to be the easier course at present; let not his name be invoked, either, if one still, for one's child, considers English a more important study than the *Shastras*, or if one continues to value Matriculation or a B.A. above *dharma*.' (Marco Pallis, ibid.)

the left hand what the right has built up. A particularly harmful aspect of this levelling out is a direct or indirect contempt for the hierarchies willed by God, or for the symbols and institutions of God in a general way, as if one could pass beyond dogma from below its level and as if love could be made perfect without respect for traditional values in so far as they represent Revelation. It is not enough to know that dogmas have a limitative character, it is necessary also to understand that they have a positive value, not only through their metaphysical and mystical contents which link them with eternal truths, but also through their purely human opportuneness, social, psychological and so forth, as foreseen by the divine Wisdom and Mercy. In any case, it cannot be admitted that all love is impeccable and that here below there are differences only of quantity, as if behind some enthusiasm or other there might not be lurking all the sterile indolence of the man who despises the sacred framework and replaces it with a concocted zeal of his own. If it is necessary to base oneself *a priori* on the formal elements of tradition, that is because it is not possible to pass beyond the world of forms without finding some point of support on the formal plane itself; none come to the 'Father' except by the 'Son', as the Gospel puts it. The *sannyâsî* abandons rites, certainly, but he abandons them ritually and does not propose that anyone so choosing should abandon them just anyhow; the *sannyâsî* is casteless, and is able to take no account of castes, but he does not dream of preaching their abolition.[1]

We could also express ourselves in another way: the modern 'spirituality' of India, whether it bases itself on *bhakti* or *jnâna* or both at once—not to mention those who think they can do better than the sages of old—this 'spirituality', we say, is characterised, not only by a too unilateral confidence in such or

[1] In Japan, the devotees of *nembutsu* abandon other practices, not because they despise them, but because, believing themselves to be fallen and incapable, they despise themselves. In Hesychasm, the monk or the hermit who has advanced in the 'Jesus Prayer' or in invocation of the name of Jesus alone, can be exempted from attending services, but this is clearly not equivalent to rejecting them.

such 'means', but also and above all by the fact of neglecting, with remarkable lack of consciousness, the human foundations —the 'human climate' it might be said[1]—the integrity of which is guaranteed only by tradition and by the sacred. Spiritual 'short cuts' exist, certainly, and cannot but exist, since they are possible; but, being founded on pure intellection on the one hand and on a subtle and rigorous technique on the other, and on bringing into play both the constitution of the microcosm and universal analogies, such short cuts exact an intellectual preparation and a psychological conditioning anchored in the tradition, apart from which they remain ineffective, or still worse lead in the opposite direction. This is the sin committed by the protagonists of such and such a *yoga* who believe that they must offer to the least apt and the least informed people a 'purely scientific' and 'non-sectarian' 'way', 'discovered' by ancient sages but 'freed from all superstition' and all 'scholasticism', that is to say, in short, freed from all traditional safeguards and indeed from every adequate reason for existing.

Nevertheless in this order of things—but only in the sphere of *bhakti*—there are some cases where it can be asked whether such irregularities are not the work of the divine Mercy which, given the chaotic and exceptional circumstances of our time, ignores certain boundaries in order to reach hearts sunk in the very depths of ignorance and triviality; but we do not propose to treat this question in detail; it is for God alone to judge. What may well be asked, however, is whether certain advantages can counterbalance certain disadvantages, and in the majority of cases it is easy to recognise that this is not so; graces which manifest themselves despite everything—given the miseries of human ignorance—could not compensate for the progressivist

[1] Some will perhaps point out that the Amidism of Honen and of Shinran also neglects the 'human foundations', but that would be a false deduction, for in this case the basis is to be found within the civilisation of ancient Japan which excludes, like every integrally traditional civilisation, the modern tendencies to triviality, pettiness and falsification; this is an essential point.

virus which falsifies minds, and above all could not justify or
sanction it.[1] We can admit that a *bhakta* of the naive and 'child
of God' type is a victim rather than responsible once the
traditional environment is lacking, for he has 'harmlessness'
without having the 'wisdom', which, precisely, ought to be
found in the general environment, in the cultural framework
which 'thinks for him'; the simple *bhakta*, much more than
the *bhakta* of intellectual type, has the right to be a child, but he
is none the less running the risks that may result from this
condition, and more important, he makes others run them.

We have just criticised inordinate confidence in 'means'
alone; on the Christian side, there is a tendency towards the
opposite mistake of hastening to declare on every occasion that
'recipes' are ineffective, that everything depends on charity and
grace; it is however perfectly legitimate and sufficient to
describe such and such a revealed 'method' as being endowed
with the power of salvation, for the simple reason that the
putting into practice of such a method, under normal circumstances, will either be accompanied without further
question by the purifications and virtues necessary for perfection, or else will be abandoned because of its difficulty, a
difficulty not of principle, but of fact; to add that all depends on
grace is to fuss over the obvious, rather like saying that the
possibility of crossing a street depends on predestination.[2] In

[1] The fact that darkness does not comprehend it cannot prevent the
shining of the light, provided that the possibility of some good exists.
It may happen that a false and 'senseless' work of art conveys a
heavenly grace as if by accident; Mercy can violate certain conditions
laid down by the very nobility of grace, and this in response to the
fervour and sincerity of some particular soul and because of the
ineluctable obstacles offered by the environment in question.

[2] In an analogous order of ideas, we have read somewhere that it is
possible to love a spiritual practice as one loves a glass of wine, for
example, and that this is not true mortification, etc.; this is quite an
arbitrary overstatement, for what counts here is precisely that prayer
is not a glass of wine; the element which distinguishes it is the divine
action of which it is the vehicle; the savour of prayer can be loved
more than all else, and that is by no means such a bad thing, at least
in men of sound mind, who are the only ones who count in this

Hinduism many simple and direct expressions are elliptic, but not simplicist; what we criticise in so many modern Hindus is their forgetfulness of the indispensable 'human climate' such as exists in every society having a sacred character, and not the innate tendency of Hindus to avoid bothering over superfluous verbal precautions. In our day, Asiatics are too prone to generalise certain 'categories' and 'implications' inherent in their respective civilisations, and to attribute to mankind as a whole various qualifications resulting from their own traditional environment, whether the causes of these qualities be near at hand or remote; this is the result of a kind of 'optical illusion' deriving above all from lack of experience, lack of terms of comparison and an inability to stand back from oneself. Asiatics have difficulty in conceiving to what extent modern Westerners differ from them, just as, generally speaking, they take little account of all that is implied psychologically by the objects and activities characterising the world of the machine and of the demagogue; a candid and impeccable logic is quite ineffectual in this order of things.[1]

*

respect. We are the last to deny that it may be necessary ultimately to transcend this kind of attachment like all others; we go indeed much further and say that it is necessary, in principle and on condition of possessing the corresponding sapiential vocation, to transcend attachment to every 'mythology' and to renounce all such 'consolation'.

[1] Paradoxically enough this lack of discernment, or this need to glorify what one cannot avoid, is to be found in all religious circles, and is due to a mentality grown largely profane and also a certain 'inferiority complex'. One would think that many believers had never heard of the prophecies concerning the end of the world and the reign of Antichrist, or that they cannot read. To the reproach of 'having pretensions to divine wisdom whilst excelling in knowledge of things of this world' (William of the Holy Love), St. Thomas Aquinas replies quite justly: 'They doubtless hold a false opinion who pretend that it is indifferent, with regard to the truth of faith, whether one has such or such a thought about the creation, provided one has a right opinion about God: for an error concerning the creation gives birth to false knowledge about God.' It is here a question of the immediate qualitative knowledge of phenomena and not of their scientific analysis: it

In order to understand certain errors of neo-bhaktism, or of neo-Hinduism in general,[1] it is necessary to recall that unfortunately the opposition between 'orthodoxy' and 'heterodoxy' does not always coincide with the opposition between 'piety' and 'worldliness'; this paradox is a favourite haunt of Satan, for there he finds a fruitful ground for all sorts of seductions and hypocrisies; it amounts, in short, to dishonest speculation on the difference of plane separating doctrinal truth from virtue. Nothing is more agreeable to the Evil One than the cries of indignation of the heretic against the occasional vice of the orthodox, or the pharisaical condemnation, by some orthodox-minded person, of a spiritual value not properly understood; the genesis of the modern West and the easy and rapid modernisation of the East are largely to be explained in terms of these inseparable oscillations. The rhythm of universal decadence, that some call 'History', proceeds by reactions: it comprises a first movement: the transforming of legitimate things into caricatures, then a second movement: reacting against these caricatures from below by abolishing their positive content, replacing by errors the truths that they disfigure. Again, heretics of every kind give to partial truths an absolute significance, which is the very definition of error; but in our day

matters, not to know that the earth turns round the sun, nor to grasp the molecular structure of matter, but to discern the cosmic value—orientated towards the absolute Cause—of the phenomena which surround us, and according to the way that they surround us. However that may be, what we wish to refute is the outlook of those who consider that it does not matter if one believes in evolution, in progress, in science and in the machine, provided one sanctifies oneself; but to believe in evolution with all that this implies is evidently to have a false opinion 'on the subject of creation'; the aberrations of Father Teilhard de Chardin show clearly how such opinions ruin 'sacred science' by implication, for they cut it off from the light in advance.

[1] It must be emphasised that in all these considerations it is not a question of the strictly traditional spirituality of India, always supposing this remains wholly intact, nor exclusively of specifically modernist movements, which as such have no interest for us, but of the contamination of the Hindu spirit by modern ideas and tendencies and hence of a state of affairs that is fluid and hard to define.

error is excused on the ground that a partial truth must of necessity be discoverable in it. In the same order of ideas, but from a somewhat different point of view, we would wish to draw attention to the following: when one feels astonishment at the foundering of the oriental civilisations, one is inclined to forget that the immense majority of men are 'worldly' and not 'spiritual', and that modern civilisation—the only civilisation to be 'worldly' *per se*—must exercise a veritable fascination over worldly men who are still living under a theocracy; the converse holds true for Westerners endowed with unusual aptitude for contemplation, who discover Asia, and then go on to rediscover Christianity with all it contains that is 'Asiatic' and timeless. The decline of the oriental civilisations is explained also by the fact that tradition—accidentally and through human weakness— does present an aspect of constraint, narrowness, routine, and even unintelligence, so that modernism readily appears to the 'worldly' under the fallacious guise of freedom, universality, greatness, not to mention 'sincerity' which is all too often merely a form of cynicism devoid of all charity; underlying all this there is an immense illusion—such as would prefer a healthy dog to a leprous saint—as well as a blind incapacity to distinguish triviality from nobility. The evils of the old civilisations are inevitable as collective facts, but escape from them must be 'upwards' and not 'downwards'.[1]

Of all this, contemporary spirituality needs to be aware, above all when it lacks vocation for the critical sense. To sum up, we would formulate our ideas as follows: if truth is a good, and even the most precious good for a being endowed with intelligence, charity cannot dispense with it. True charity will, so far as is possible, seek to give only unmixed good and to offer to every man the nourishment that suits him best, be it

[1] There are neo-Hindu 'reformers' who want to 'reject all these fables about cults, this blowing of conches, this ringing of bells', and even 'all pride of knowledge and study of the *Shastras*, and all those methods for attaining personal deliverance. . . .' But if the Brahmans had not blown conches during thousands of years, none of you 'reformers' of India today would even exist!

'dogmatic' or 'dualistic' as some would say[1]; this sort of charity is always conscious of its responsibilities and does not launch out into a short-sighted and two-edged idealism; it never forgets the weaknesses of human nature, nor the needs—as well as the dangers—resulting from it, which every traditional wisdom has foreseen far better than man with his most generous dreams could ever do.

[1] Those who consider the fact of seeing evil to be a proof of wickedness ('the good see nothing but good everywhere', etc.) are the first to see evil once it is a question of orthodoxy, dogmas, cults, priestly institutions; in practice it is evil itself which profits most from their cult of 'universal Love'.

5

The Doctrine of Illusion

It may seem strange that it should be necessary to point out that the metaphysical doctrine of illusion is not just a solution of convenience which justifies bringing everything on the plane of phenomena to a single level. Certainly, reality is reality and illusion is illusion; but no 'realisation' warrants the belief that two and two make five or that black is white, on the pretext that numbers and colours are illusory. None the less there is a weakness here, which is liable to appear in the shadow of 'operative' *jnâna* and which tends, when confronted with the nature of things, to reduce everything to a single intellectual and experimental motif, thus blurring all qualitative differences, whereas in reality the function of the Intellect is just the reverse, for it discriminates 'externally' to the extent that it unifies 'internally'; metaphysical synthesis is not a physical levelling out.[1] This so-called Vedantic levelling out becomes particularly troublesome when it attacks sacred things that it judges to be inferior: when, for example, it loses sight of the fact that religion, which it labels 'sectarianism', is not of human origin and that there are things which, though on a level below that of supreme knowledge, are none the less the will of God and not inventions of man; the miracles of Christ are not 'occult powers' (*siddhis*) that can be exercised or not exercised, but divine manifestations, hence also facts that elude all psychological evaluation, and Christ is not a man who became wise,

---

[1] If 'clay and gold are one', as Ramakrishna declared after a mystical experience and basing himself moreover on the Scriptures, it is obvious that this statement is valid in the spiritual sense, but not on the physical plane; there is in fact no difference between precious and common materials when one is placed at the subjective point of view of detachment or at the objective point of view of the limits of existence; but these surpassing degrees cannot be realised if one starts by repudiating differences on their own plane; the sublime is not to be sought in absurdities.

but Wisdom become man.[1] That all is *Atmâ*—or *Mâyâ*,
according to the point of view—clearly does not authorise us
to 'take a rope for a snake', as the Vedantists say; quite the
contrary; once again, there is no true synthesis without discernment. What is *Vedânta* if not 'discrimination' (*viveka*)
between the real and the unreal, and an investigation (*vichâra*)
into our true nature? But discrimination in the 'vertical
direction' (between *Sachchidânanda* and *nama-rûpa*) does not
go without an equivalent discrimination in the 'horizontal
direction', concerning the 'qualities' (*gunas*).

Certain theorists of the *Vedânta*, anxious to buttress their
conviction of the exclusive reality of the Self, 'inner Witness' of
all thought, find it necessary to deny the reality of the object as
if it were 'mind' that creates the objective world—the Scriptures
teach the contrary[2]—and as if one term of a polarity had any
kind of meaning without the opposite and complementary term.
In thus reducing the object to the subject, no explanation is
given either of the cause of the world, or of its homogeneity
which makes all men see the same sun and not something else.
The only valid argument is forgotten, namely that the world is
the illusion, not of each particular individual—otherwise each
individual would dream a different world—but of a collectivity
or a plurality of collectivities which are superimposed on or
penetrate one another; this 'collective subject' embraces all
humanity, and, on a vaster scale, all the creatures of the earth.
The empirical homogeneity of the world is then explained by
solidarity within a cosmic dream, marked by a common
'sensibility'; a mountain is a mountain and not a dream, even
for an ant, or it would be in the void that ants would be cross-

[1] No doubt it is necessary to leave out of account such judgements as
are to be explained either by a 'traditionally legitimate' ignorance, or
by a revealed perspective giving grounds for a particular interpretation
of such and such symbolical facts; this second possibility in any case
concerns Semites rather than Hindus.

[2] 'Thus, appearances (external objects) are not caused by mind, nor
is mind the product of appearances.' (*Mândûkya-Kârikâ* of Gaudapada,
IV, 54.) Shankarâchârya takes up this thesis in his commentary.

ing rocks and climbing slopes. There is then a multiform 'earthly being' which is a state of existence having innumerable degrees or 'compartments', the centre of which is the human state: all the subjects contained in this collective subject will have homogeneous reactions, in the sense that for all of them the sun gives heat, light and life, or that for all a rock is impenetrable, and so forth. This 'being' must moreover extend beyond the limits of the earth, for it is more than probable that this something that causes us the sensation 'sun', causes the same sensation to extra-terrestrial beings, so that the problem of objectivity—or the collective dream—scarcely stops at the limits of any given subjective universe; a particular cosmos is a closed system only in a relative sense, for Existence is one. It is, in fact, only the total Universe that we can qualify as 'dream' pure and simple, since an ordinary dream presupposes by definition a perfect subjectivity and this condition, which implies that vision should be shared by no other subject— unless it be by subjective coincidence—is fulfilled only in the 'dream' of the universal Soul, where the subject is unique; in this case, the word 'dream' is only another term for 'illusion' or for *mâyâ*.[1] The starfilled sky is a dream, not in so far as we see it or all men see it, but in so far as the universal Soul 'conceives' it in a play that is eternally free and has no other motif than Beatitude; the starry vault is an 'imagination' not of our individual consciousness, but of a 'universal layer' of our consciousness, hence of a consciousness which immensely exceeds the *ego*, whence the homogeneity of the empirical world. It is 'universal Man' who dreams,[2] and we dream in him and with him.

In other terms: for the Absolute, there is no difference

---

[1] Let us note that *mâyâ* possesses not only the aspect of 'illusion', but also that of 'universal unfolding', 'divine art', 'cosmic magic'; but in the end, its meaning of illusion is incontestable, since to believe in the absolute reality of the *ego* and of the world is, according to the Vedantists, an effect of 'ignorance'.

[2] Or *Viraj*, the divine Intelligence in so far as it 'conceives' the physical world.

between objects perceived in the waking state or in the dream state; but from the point of view of relative reality—which we cannot hold to be nonexistent since we find ourselves in it and act on that basis—there is between these two states an eminent difference, in the sense that the first state has more universality —hence more reality—than the second. The proof: firstly, external objects are perceived by several subjects, and even by innumerable subjects in space and time, according to circumstances, whilst in dream there is only a single subject, who in reality is at the same time object since he creates the images out of his own substance; secondly, external objects can themselves be subjects, and in this case it is evident *a priori* that the fact of being perceived by anyone at all neither adds nor subtracts anything in relation to their reality; thirdly, those who profess an absolute indistinction between waking and dream states know, when they are awake, that the world is illusory, which they cannot know when they are asleep, and this proves that, for the subject equally, the waking state excels, in its degree of universality, the cloudy state of dream; fourthly, those who profess an absolute indistinction between the two states behave as if they did not believe in it, since they eat, talk, and run when chased by a bull. Objection will no doubt be made that the sage should not concern himself with relative reality and therefore with degrees of universality; we reply yes, he must, since he is concerned with it in all kinds of ways, which deprives him of any right to claim to consider the Absolute exclusively; whoever has eyes and ears is obliged to discern relativities, with or without spiritual vision of *Atmâ*. If a man dreams of eating, he has the excuse of not acting freely or in full lucidity[1]; but if he eats when awake, while denying the qualitative ontological difference between the two states in an

---

[1] A prayer or an invocation made in sleep however has merit, whereas sin committed in dream does not count, which shows that the divine Mercy does not admit of symmetry between good and evil, and also that dreaming has a unilateral aspect of reality, just as the waking state has an aspect of dream or of illusion.

unconditional sense, he has no excuse, since he believes he is
dreaming and knows that the dream is illusory; he should not
then perform voluntarily actions the sole excuse for which, in
dream, is that they are involuntary. Moreover, in dreams it
happens to all of us to work all sorts of wonders: jumping over
precipices and floating happily in the void like a bird, and so on;
let him who believes that all is dream and mere subjectivity do
half as much in the waking state, if he is sincere! If the opinion
which unconditionally confuses the states of waking and of
dreaming were well founded and if these two states were
equivalent precisely on the plane of relativity—whilst in reality
they are so only in the sight of the Absolute—it would be
indifferent whether a man was a sage dreaming he was a fool, or
a fool dreaming he was a sage.

The great question to be asked here is: who is the subject?[1]
The fact that we have no possibility of making a mountain cease
to exist—as we can sometimes do in a dream—proves that our
particular 'I', while being for the mountain an accidental
subject, is none the less not the creative subject on which the
mountain, *qua* illusion, depends: it also proves that the mountain, though quite illusory on the plane of the universal subject
and from the point of view of Intellect, none the less possesses
a relative reality for our *ego*, and even has more reality than our
imaginations. Once again, it is not possible in sound logic that
a man should both deny that Reality, as well as being absolute,
comprises degrees, and that he should at the same time accept
the fact that he exists and that in consequence he acts; one

---

[1] The *de facto* ambiguity of this question is in part explained by the
fact that the Hindus, who knew what was implied in such matters,
have never in their expositions, which are deliberately elliptical and
centred on the essential, gone out of their way to offer precisions
which seemed to them pointless; but one must not take dialectical
syntheses for mere simplifications and draw absurd conclusions from
the doctrine of illusion, an error of which the ancient followers of
Vedanta were clearly not guilty, or they would have been common
solipsists. Schopenhauer was wrong in thinking that solipsism is
logically irrefutable, but right in declaring solipsists to be ripe for
the lunatic asylum.

cannot at the same time both exist and deny Existence, or act and deny the cause of activity.

Now, if we cannot admit that the world is only the product of our mind (caused by what?) no more can we admit that the evil we discern in the world is only an objectivation of our own defects (in respect of what?) and that for the good man all is good. If the end of it all is to be an abdication of intelligence, coupled with a facile and inoperative monism, it is useless to resort to a 'way of knowledge'. It is true that 'evil', or what we call such, reduces itself in the last analysis to a tendency which cannot not be and is part of the universal equilibrium; but this does not prevent there being, on the plane of cosmic coagulations—whether it be a question of the 'external' world or of the soul—phenomena which are either conformable, or contrary to pure Being (*Sat*, whence *sattwa*), or mean that creatures endowed with understanding should fail to recognise them; to affirm the contrary is to disavow all the sacred Scriptures, not to mention simple common sense. In metaphysics, as in every other realm, it is necessary to know how to put everything in its place.

As for the question of the 'origin' of illusion, it is among those questions that can be resolved—or rather, there is nothing in it to resolve—though this resolution cannot be adjusted to suit all needs of causality; there are demonstrations which, whether they are understood or not, are sufficient in themselves and indeed constitute pillars of metaphysical doctrine. Let us limit ourselves here to recalling what we have already said elsewhere,[1] namely that the infinitude of Reality implies the possibility of its own negation, and that, this negation being impossible in the Absolute itself, it is necessary that this 'possibility of the impossible' should be realised in an 'internal dimension' which is 'neither real nor unreal', that is to say

[1] In *Spiritual Perspectives and Human Facts.* Faber, 1954. We believe that a certain repetition in our writings can only add to their clarity, given the importance or the difficulty of the subjects treated; repetition is moreover inevitable in matters of this kind.

which is real on its own level while being unreal in respect of Essence, with the result that we touch everywhere the Absolute, from which we cannot emerge, although it is at the same time infinitely far off, so that no thought can ever circumscribe it.

GNOSIS

6

Gnosis, Language of the Self

There are various ways of expressing or defining the difference between gnosis and love—or between *jnâna* and *bhakti*—but here we wish to consider one criterion only, and it is this: for the 'volitional' or 'affective' man (the *bhakta*) God is 'He' and the *ego* is 'I', whereas for the 'gnostic' or 'intellective' man (the *jnâni*)[1] God is 'I'—or 'Self'—and the *ego* is 'he' or 'other'.[2] It will also be immediately apparent why it is the former and not the latter perspective that determines all religious dogmatism: it is because the majority of men start out from certainty about the *ego* rather than about the Absolute. Most men are individualists and consequently but little suited to make 'a concrete abstraction' of their empirical 'I', a process which is an intellectual and not a moral one: in other words, few have the gift of impersonal contemplation—for it is of this that we are speaking—such as will allow 'God to think in us', if such an expression is permissible. The nature of pure intellection will be better understood from considering the following: Intellect, which is One, presents itself in three

[1] We would as readily have said 'the theosopher', but this word might give rise to confusions. That the terms 'gnostic' or 'theosopher' should have fallen into discredit is a bad sign, not, certainly, for men like Clement of Alexandria or Boehme who used them, but for that world which has occasioned and sanctioned such discredit. The same applies to the word 'intellectual', the meaning of which has become quite trivial. As for the term 'pneumatic', it applies, seemingly, to realisation alone, not to theory.

[2] It is true that most of the sapiential doctrines, in taking account of the *ego* as a fact and inasmuch as they conform to 'the letter' of the Revelation from which they derive, refer to the Absolute as 'He', as do the 'dualists' of the way of love, but this is hardly more than a question of dialectic which in no way modifies the fundamental perspective, as we have explained elsewhere (*Spiritual Perspectives and Human Facts*, section on *Vedanta*). Moreover the *Advaita Vedanta*, which is the most direct possible expression of gnosis, does not exclude 'objectivist' formulations of the Principle, such as *Brahma*, *Shiva* and other divine Names.

fundamental aspects—at least in so far as we are situated in the 'separative illusion' as is the case for every creature as such—namely, first the divine Intellect, which is Light and pure Act; secondly the cosmic Intellect, which is a receptacle or mirror in relation to God and light in relation to man; and thirdly the human Intellect, which is a mirror in relation to both of the foregoing and light in relation to the individual soul[1]; one must be careful, therefore, to distinguish in the Intellect—the divine Intellect excepted—an 'uncreated' aspect which is essential and a 'created' aspect which is 'accidental' or rather 'contingent'.[2] This synthetic view of things 'results', one might say, from the principle of non-alterity: that which is not 'other' in any respect whatsoever is 'identical' under the relationship here being considered, so much so that intelligence as such—whether it be the intelligence of a man conforming to truth or that of a plant causing it irresistibly to turn towards the light—'is' the intelligence of God; intelligence is only 'human' or 'vegetable' in relation to specific limitations, and similar considerations apply to every positive quality, and therefore to all virtues, which are always those of God, not of course in the accidental conditions that narrow their scope, but in their content or essence.

*

From these considerations it can be seen that the great Gospel virtues—charity, humility, poverty, childlikeness—have their final end in the 'Self'[3]: they represent so many negations of that

[1] Words of the Gospel such as 'I am the light of the world' or 'No man cometh to the Father but by me' are applicable in all these three senses.

[2] The mystery of 'universal Spirit' (*Er-Rûh*) consists, in Islam, in not being able to say of it either that it is 'created' or that it is 'uncreated'; the same mystery is to be met with in that Intellect we have called 'human' and which Meister Eckhart defined in an ambiguous manner.

[3] The same could be said of the commandments of the Decalogue: in a final analysis each one of them marks an aspect of the Self and each transgression likewise reveals an aspect of the *ego* as such. The 'chosen

ontological 'bubble' which is the *ego*, negations that are not
individualist and thereby contradictory,[1] but intellective; that
is, their point of departure is the very Self, in conformity with
the most profound nature of things. In a similar way, if a sage
cannot be satisfied, in a final sense, with any created bliss—
'the (created) Paradise is a prison for the Sufi'—this is not due
to any pretention or ingratitude on his part, far from it, but
simply because the Intellect tends towards its own Source, or
because the Self in us 'wants to be delivered'. If Christ 'is
God', that is because the Intellect—'come down from Heaven'
—'is the Self'; and in that sense, all genuine religions are
'Christian': each one postulates, on the one hand, the uncreated
Intellect—or the Logos, 'uncreated Word' of God, which
comes to the same thing if one takes into account the 'radiation'
of Intellect—and on the other hand it postulates the earthly
manifestation of that Word and the deliverance procured
through it; every complete tradition postulates, in the final
analysis, extinction of the *ego* in favour of the divine 'I', an
extinction for which the sacred Law provides an elementary
framework, though the Law must remain 'dualistic' in its
common letter to meet the needs of the majority and consequently for reasons of social psychology. 'Internally' every
religion is the doctrine of the one Self and its earthly manifestation, as also the way leading to the abolition of the false
self, or the way of the mysterious reintegration of our 'personality' in the celestial Prototype; 'externally' the religions
amount to 'mythologies' or, to be more exact, to symbolisms
designed for differing human receptacles and displaying, by

people' corresponds to the soul that is 'naturally' idolatrous and
rebellious but has been 'supernaturally' redeemed by the Messiah, who
is Grace or Intellect.

[1] The complex of a false guiltiness and the dessication of a false
humility are the commonest expressions of this contradiction. An
attitude is false in proportion as it runs counter to truth; true humility,
the kind that is most efficacious, is an impersonal 'non-pride' which
remains independent of the alternative 'humiliation—flattery' and
avoids all unhealthy pre-occupation with the 'I'. Fundamental virtues
are centred in God, not in man.

this limitation, not a contradiction *in divinis* but on the contrary a mercy. A doctrine or a Way is exoteric in proportion to the need for it to take account of individualism—which is the fruit not so much of passion itself as of the hold exerted by passion upon thought—and to veil the equation of 'Intellect' and 'Self' under a mythological or moral 'imagery', and that irrespective of whether an historical element is combined in that imagery or not: and a doctrine is esoteric in proportion as it communicates the very essence of our universal position, our situation midway between nothingness and Infinity. Esotericism looks to the nature of things and not merely to our human eschatology; it views the Universe not from the human standpoint but 'from the standpoint of God'.[1]

The exoteric mentality, with its one-sided logic and its somewhat passion-tainted 'rationality', scarcely conceives that there are questions to which the answer is at once 'yes' and 'no'; it is always afraid of 'falling' into 'dualism', 'pantheism', 'quietism' or something of the kind. In metaphysics as in psychology it is sometimes necessary to resort to ambiguous answers; for example, to the question: the world, 'is it' God? we reply: 'no', if by the 'world' is understood ontological manifestation as such, that is to say in its aspect of existential or demiurgic relativity; 'yes', if by 'world' is understood manifestation in so far as it is causally or substantially divine, since nothing can be outside of God; in the first case, God is exclusive and transcendent Principle, and in the second, total Reality or universal and inclusive Substance. God alone 'is'; the world

---

[1] 'It is for certain chosen men, who have been allowed to pass from faith to gnosis, that the sacred mysteries of wisdom have been preserved under the veil of parables' (Clement of Alexandria, *Stromata*, VI, 126). This means, not that the parables do not contain a sense which is designed for all Christians while having to be hidden provisionally from unbelievers, but that they are at the same time the vehicles of a sense that is genuinely gnostic or metaphysical, and thereby incomprehensible to the majority of Christians themselves. Christ's command not to cast pearls before swine nor to give what is sacred to dogs cannot have a meaning that is merely limited in time and reduced to a question of what is externally opportune.

is a limited 'divine aspect', for it cannot—if we are to avoid absurdity—be a nothingness on its own level. To affirm on the one hand that the world has no 'divine quality', and on the other that it is real apart from God and that it never ceases so to be, amounts to admitting two Divinities, two Realities, two Absolutes.

That which is 'incarnation' for Christianity is 'revelation' or 'descent' for the other two monotheistic religions. The truth that only the divine manifestation 'is the Self', to the exclusion of every human counterfeit, becomes exoterically: only such and such a divine manifestation—to the exclusion of all others— is the Self. It could also be said, on the plane of the microcosm, that the Intellect alone, and no other human faculty, is the Self—not reason nor imagination nor memory nor feeling nor the faculties of sensory perception—although, viewed as existential structure, everything reflects or 'is' the Self in some way or another. This exclusive value attaching to 'incarnation' plainly also bears, besides its spiritual significance, a literal meaning historically, which applies when one considers the particular human cosmos where this divine manifestation has taken place, that is to say, in the case of Christ, the world of the Roman Empire and, in a still larger sense, the world of those whom the particular grace of Christ has 'chosen', regardless of their country of origin; but the literalist interpretation becomes unacceptable whenever an attempt is made to add some fact or other, be it even a sacred fact, to metaphysical truth, as if the latter were incomplete without it—whereas all possible facts are already included in that truth—and as if metaphysical truth were subject to time. To take a second example: the Koranic affirmation that 'God alone is God' means that there is no Self but the Self; exoterically however this statement implies that God could not manifest Himself as such 'outside Himself', which amounts to rejecting the phenomenon of 'incarnation'; but in every case of this kind, esotericism 're-stores' the total truth on the plane of principles. In fact, the essential difference between Christian and Islamic gnosis is this: whereas Christian gnosis projects the mystery of the Man-God—and thereby the mystery of the Trinity—into the soul of the gnostic, as is shown, for example, by certain Eckhartian texts, Sufism, for its part, sees 'unification' (*tawhid*) or the 'unity of Existence' or, better still, the unity of Universal Reality (*wahdat El-Wujûd*, sometimes translated as 'Supreme Identity') as rising from the very nature of the Divine Unity.[1]

The exoteric distinction between 'the true religion' and 'false religions' is replaced, for the gnostic, by the distinction between gnosis and beliefs, or between essence and forms.[2] The sapiential perspective alone is an esotericism in the absolute sense, or in other words, it alone is necessarily and integrally esoteric, because it alone reaches beyond all relativities.

The way of love is more or less esoteric as seen from the angle of social religion, and more or less exoteric as seen from the angle of gnosis, and this moreover explains certain somewhat ambiguous aspects of Christianity; but one must take care not to confuse the aspect 'love' in gnosis itself with doctrines and methods of a specifically *bhaktic*, and therefore 'dualist' and emotive character.

*

God is 'Light' 'before' He is 'Heat', if it may be so expressed;

[1] The Islamic formula *Lâ ilaha illâ Llâh* means, according to gnosis, that 'there is no "me" except it be I'—therefore no real or positive *ego* except the Self—a meaning which springs from expressions such as the *Anâ-l-Haqq* ('I am the Truth') of El Hallaj or the *Subhânî* ('Glory to Me') of Bayezid. The Prophet himself enunciated the same mystery in the following terms: 'He who has seen me, has seen the Truth (God)', (that is to say: God cannot be seen except through His receptacle or, in a more general but less direct sense, through His symbol), and also: 'I am He and He is I, save that I am who I am, and He is who He is'.—'I have been charged with fulfilling my mission since the best of the ages of Adam (the origin of the world), from one age to another until this age where I am.'

[2] If in relation to the pole 'subject' gnosis is the doctrine of the Self, in relation to the pole 'object' it will be the doctrine of the Essence: "That knowledge which sees the one Indestructible in all beings, the One Indivisible in all separate lives, may be truly called Pure Knowledge' (*Sattwa*, the 'luminous' or 'upwards' tendency). (*Bhagavad-Gîtâ*, XVIII, 20, translated by Shri Purohit Swami. Faber, 1935.)

gnosis 'precedes' love, or rather, love 'follows' gnosis, since the latter includes love after its own fashion, whereas love is not other than the bliss that has 'come forth' from gnosis. One can love something false, without love ceasing to be what it is; but one cannot 'know' falsehood in a similar way, that is to say knowledge cannot be under illusion as to its object without ceasing to be what it is; error always implies a privation of knowledge, whereas sin does not imply a privation of will. Therein lies a most important application of the symbolism of the Adamic 'androgyne' and of the creation of Eve: it is only after the 'coming forth' of love outside knowledge—whence the polarisation of 'intelligence' and 'will'—that the temptation and fall could—or can—take place; in one sense, the rational faculty became detached from Intellect through the intrusion of will, seduced by 'the serpent' and rendered 'free' from below, that is to say rendered capable of making choice between true and false; choice of falsehood having once become possible, it was bound to present itself as a seduction of torrential force; reason, mother of the 'wisdom according to the flesh' is the 'natural child' issued from Adam's sin. Here the serpent represents what Hindus understand by *tamas*,[1] that tendency which is 'downward', 'towards obscurity', 'compressive' and at the same time 'dispersive' and 'dissolving' and which on contact with the human becomes personified as Satan. The question: 'why does evil exist?' amounts, to all intents and purposes, to asking why there is an existence; the serpent is to be found in Paradise because Paradise exists. Paradise without the serpent would be God.

*

[1] The negative aspects of *tamas* which are here in question are but half the story: under its positive aspect *tamas* can also act as a principle of stability, in the absence of which no world could hold together, nor any object or being endure for a moment. It is a common mistake to regard *tamas* as tantamount to evil or ignorance as such, whereas it is one of the constituent qualities of Existence, affecting everything contained therein in continually varying proportions, and this is true of things whether they are deemed beneficial or harmful. (Note to the English edition.)

Man complains of his sufferings, such as separation and death; but has he not inflicted them *a priori* upon the Self, by his very egoity? Is not individuation a separation from the divine 'I' and is not the *ego* itself a death in respect of infinite Life? It will be objected that we are not responsible for our existence; but man ceaselessly recreates, in his actions, this responsibility which he thinks he does not have; in this, taken together with the foregoing considerations, lies the deeper meaning of original sin.[1] Man suffers because he wishes to be 'self' in opposition to 'Self', and Christ effaces this fundamental 'sin' by taking on Himself its resultant suffering. He is the Self holding out a hand to 'me'; man must 'lose his life', the life of the *ego*, in order to keep it, the life of the Self. Under His solar aspect—implying the warmth of love as also the light of wisdom—Christ is the Self that unites and absorbs all beings. The Self became *ego* in order that the *ego* might become Self; the divine 'Subject' became cosmic 'object' because 'object' must once again become 'subject'.[2] The Self alone is 'itself'; the

[1] There are some apparent heresies that are not false in themselves, but refer to an 'ontological stratum' lying deeper than that of ordinary theological concepts: the refusal to attribute an absolute validity to 'original sin' proceeds, when it has an adequate motive, from a more fundamental and more 'neutral' vision of our human reality, one which however is less accessible to a given mentality and therefore also less opportune for a given morality; similarly, 'quietism', in so far as it contains a legitimate element, stands nearer to contemplation and gnosis than does the accumulating of merits; 'there is no lustral water like unto Knowledge' says the Law of Manu. It can be regretted, without departing from realism, that Western theology has not known a grading of truths according to differing levels of validity: having chosen but one level, or more or less so, namely the level of what was opportune for the collectivity, this theology firstly impoverished itself and then indirectly provoked 'explosions' which have ended by threatening its very existence.

[2] 'And the light shineth in darkness; and the darkness comprehended it not': the *ego* has not understood that its own immortal reality—or that of the Intellect—is none other than the Self. 'Inasmuch as ye have done it unto one of the least of these my brethren, ye have done it unto me': this is the enunciation, as Coomaraswamy so justly remarked, of the cosmic reverberation of the Self, who is 'the one and only trans-migrant' according to Shankara.

ego is 'other', hence its initial unbalance and its insatiability: it never ceases its search for itself; in whatever it does, it is in pursuit of that transcendent and absolute 'Me' in which the beatitudes are intrinsic and permanent instead of being scattered about a world that is endlessly deceitful. 'The Kingdom of God is within you.'

If 'that which is born of the Spirit is spirit', this is because Spirit is Self and because there is no other knowing or loving Subject in the infinite Blessedness; similarly, if he that is 'born of the Spirit'[1] is like the wind of which thou 'canst not tell whence it cometh, and whither it goeth', this is because, being identified with the Self, he is without origin[2]; he has come forth from the chain of cosmic causations and dwells in the Changeless. Similarly again, a reference to the Self—apart from other meanings—is to be seen in these words: 'No man hath ascended up to heaven, but he that came down from heaven . . .'. To 'ascend up to heaven' is to 'become One-self', that is to say, to become that which one had never really ceased to be, in the sense that the essence of the *ego* is the Self, that 'Life' that we can only purchase by losing the life of 'me'.[3]

---

[1] 'Except a man be born of water and of the Spirit, he cannot enter into the kingdom of God. That which is born of the flesh is flesh; and that which is born of the Spirit is spirit' (John iii, 5–6)—'Water is looked on by many traditions as the original medium of beings, and the reason lies in its symbolism . . . by which water represents *Mula Prakriti*; in a superior sense and by transposition, water is Universal Possibility itself; he that is 'born of water' becomes a 'son of the Virgin', therefore also an adopted brother of Christ and co-heir of the Kingdom of God. Besides, if one observes the fact that 'spirit' . . . is the Hebrew *Ruahh* (here associated with water as a complementary principle, as at the beginning of Genesis) and that *Ruahh* at the same time corresponds to air, one will recognise in this the idea of purification by the elements. . . .' (René Guénon, *Man and his Becoming according to the Vedanta*, Chapter XX, footnote.)

[2] 'Whence come these Buddhas? Whither vanishes this body of mine? Reflecting thus he sees that all the Tathâgatas come from nowhere and go no-where.' *Pratyutpanna-Samâdhi-Sûtra*, quoted by Suzuki in *Essays on Zen Buddhism: The Kô-an and the Nembutsu*.

[3] 'With Christ I must be buried,' said St. Gregory of Nazianza,

For Plato's Socrates, the 'true philosopher' is he who consecrates himself to 'studying the separation of soul from body, or the liberation of the soul', and 'who is always occupied in the practice of dying'; it is he who withdraws from the bodily—and therefore from all which, in the *ego*, is the shadow or echo of the surrounding world—in order to be no more than absolutely pure soul, immortal Soul, Self: 'The Soul-in-itself must contemplate Things-in-themselves' (Phaedo). Thus the criterion of truth—and the basis of conviction, this reverberation of Light in the 'outer man'—is Truth in itself, the pre-phenomenal Intelligence by which 'all things were made' and without which 'was not anything made that was made'.

*

We have said previously that, in the human microcosm, only the Intellect 'is' the Self, and not any specifically 'mental' faculty. For just as a distinction has to be made between an ordinary creature and 'the Word made flesh', so also it is necessary to distinguish between rational thought, which is discursive and proceeds from the mental faculty alone, and intellective thought, which proceeds from intuition and pure Intellect: this second mode of thought is, in effect, an 'exteriorisation resulting from an interiorisation', whereas the first is purely and simply an expression resulting from manifestation as such. To rational thought there corresponds the infra-human world, production of the 'cosmic brain', and to intellective thought there corresponds the human race, expression of the 'heart'; on a smaller scale and within the framework of humanity itself, it is the *Avatâra* who corresponds to this

'with Christ I must rise again, and with Christ I must inherit; I must become Son of God and God himself.' (Sermon, VII, 23.) 'Understand who has given you to be Son of God, heir of Christ, and—to use a bold term—God himself.' (Ibid., XIV, 23.) 'But this (the Kingdom of Heaven) consists, in my view, in nothing but the possession of what is most pure and most perfect. But the most perfect thing that exists is Knowledge of God.' (Ibid., XX, 12.)

second mode of thought. The whole Christ-enacted drama, or the drama of Revelation unqualified, is thus prefigured—or else 'post-figured', according to the point of view—in the intellectual act, either in the original intellection itself or in unitive meditation; this form of thought is like a 'redemptive' or 'unitive incarnation' of the Heart-Intellect. In other words, a distinction has to be made between terrestrial thought, aroused by the environment and finding its term within the environment, and celestial thought aroused by that which is our eternal substance and finding its term beyond ourselves and, in the final analysis, in the Self. Reason is something like a 'profane intelligence'; essentially the profane point of view springs from there. It is necessary for reason to be determined, transfigured or regenerated, either by faith, or by gnosis which is the quintessence of faith.

Gnosis, by the very fact that it is a 'knowing' and not a 'willing', is centred in 'that which is' and not in 'that which ought to be'; from this there results a way of regarding the world and life greatly differing from the way, more 'meritorious' perhaps but less 'true', in which minds predominantly volitive regard the vicissitudes of existence. The background of the drama of life is, for the *bhakta*, the 'Will of God' and, for the *jnâni*, the nature of things; the accepting of his fate results, for the former, from unconditional love, from 'that which must be'; for the latter acceptance results from discernment of metaphysical necessity, therefore from 'that which is'. The *bhakta* accepts all fate as coming from the Beloved; he also accepts it because he makes no distinction between 'me' and 'others' and because, from this very fact, he cannot rebel against an event merely because it has happened to himself and not to some other person; if he accepts all from love of God, he also accepts, on that very basis, out of love of his neighbour. The attitude of the *jnâni*, on the other hand, is an impassibility founded upon discerning between Real and Unreal: 'the world is false, *Brahma* is true'; 'That art Thou' (*Brahma, Atmâ*); 'All is *Atmâ*'; '*I am Brahma*'. Events of life arise, as do all phenomena, out of the indefinitely varying combinations of the three 'cosmic qualities' (the *gunas*: *sattwa*, *rajas* and *tamas*); these events then cannot not be, in such measure as the world is relatively real; but as soon as that relativity is transcended, they cease to exist and then there is no longer a 'good' or an 'evil', nor any karmic causation; the plane of the *gunas* ('simultaneous' qualities) and of *karma* (made up of 'successive' qualities) is as if annihilated in the undifferentiated serenity of Being or of the Self. And similarly there is no 'juridical' relationship between the astonishments, anxieties and indignations of the soul and the unconditional serenity of Intellect, or to be more precise, between the logic of disquiet and the transcendence of dispassion; the gap is incommensurable and yet the second term is already there concealed within the first; it is, so to speak, already within reach.

In spiritual life, he who says 'to will' says 'to will Good'; 'to will Good' is 'to will well', that is to say to 'will through the Good', or 'through God'; instead of 'to will' one could also say 'to love' and instead of 'the Good' one could say 'the Beautiful'. On the other hand, he who says 'to know' says 'to know that which is'; he who says 'to know that which is', says, in a final analysis, 'to be that which knows': the Self.

*

Reference has been made to the 'cosmic qualities', the *gunas*, and to *karma*, as well as to the dispassion which transcends all conditions of existence: this dispassion—or this deliverance—lies to some extent at the centre of existence like a kernel of peace and light; it is like a drop of redemptive spray in an ocean of flames. 'The whole universe is on fire', said the Buddha; our misfortune lies in our not knowing that the substance of existence is fire—this substance into which we are woven while yet remaining alien bodies. For the 'naive' and 'unrepentant', the world is a neutral space from which he chooses the agreeable content whilst believing he has the power to avoid the disagreeable provided he is clever and has good fortune; but the man who does not know that existence is an immense brazier has no imperative reason for wanting to get out of it, and that is why an Arab proverb says 'the summit of wisdom is the fear of God'—that is to say the fear of divine afflictions, which are the price of our state of remoteness.

The kernel of light at the centre of the current of forms is essentially the 'memory of God'—which in the end demands all that we are—as the words of Muhammad declare: 'All that is to be found on earth is cursed, save only the memory of God', and: 'There is no fault greater than that of existing.' 'There is none good but one, that is, God,' said Christ: this implies that what comes from God—His Name—and what leads to Him— remembering His Name—share in His goodness. The fire, which is virtual in things, and on which we live withdraws from them to the extent that we are centred on the mystery of this remembering; things then become transparent and transmit to us the rays of their immutable and blessed archetypes. It could also be said that existence is fiery in so far as it is regarded as being outside God and, by this fact, leads to fire; it is a consuming blaze for the perverted will and illumination for the contemplative intelligence, and it is, thus, at once a threat and a 'consolation', enslaving seduction and liberating vision. It is the changeless and blessed archetypes that man is seeking when he attaches himself to shadows here below; and he suffers cruelly, first when the shadows disappear and later when, at death, he perceives the archetypes, from which his love for shadows had turned him away.[1]

In its global reality, Existence is serene and not maleficent; the cosmic Wrath is reabsorbed in total and virginal Equilibrium —Existence in itself is the universal Virgin who conquers, by her purity as also by her mercy, the sin of the demiurgic Eve, the bringer forth of creatures and of passions; Eve who brings forth, seduces and attaches, is 'eternally' conquered by the Virgin who purifies, pardons and sets free.

---

[1] Music—like dancing—is the art of bringing terrestrial shadows back to celestial vibrations and divine archetypes. In the plastic arts an analogous function is performed by stylisation.

For gnosis, the existential fire is not separable from ignorance, and so from illusion. The fundamental cause of illusion or of ignorance is not however our state of fall nor some deficiency of the existential substance, but the principle of objectivation, by which the pole 'being' is cut off from the pure Subject; seen from this angle, the universal Virgin also is 'illusory', and even Being is so in as far as it is distinct from the supra-ontological Subject which is the Self.[1] But Existence and Being, even if they are of the realm of *Mâyâ*, nonetheless remain beyond the current of forms, and in consequence beyond separation, suffering and death.

Gnosis, it must be repeated, is our participation—which may be quite precarious and conditional, yet is nonetheless possible since we could not be in every respect absolutely 'distinct' from God, otherwise we should have no reality at all—gnosis, then, is our participation in the 'perspective' of the divine Subject which, in turn, is beyond the separative polarity, 'subject-object', though this in no way signifies that it does not carry in itself, in a manner conforming with its Essence, the cause of all cosmic polarisations; this is to say that we can discern something like a polarity in it, but on condition of not seeing there any separation or opposition.

*

The absolute Subject carries its own immediate and con-natural Object within itself and that Object is infinite Blessedness. When the Hindu doctrine describes *Atmâ* as being made up of 'Being', 'Consciousness' and 'Bliss' (*Sat, Chit, Ânanda*, whence the divine Name *Sachchidânanda*) this enumeration means that the subject is 'Being that Knows, having Bliss for object': 'being'—or 'being real'—this is Consciousness of all its own possibilities. The use of the verb 'to be' here is quite provisional, since the Self is situated beyond ontological Unity.

[1] In Eckhart, Silesius, Omar Khayyam and others, allusions are found to this 'relativity' of Being in relation to the Self. In the doctrines of India and the Far East—Shivaite *Vedânta*, Mahâyâna Buddhism and Taoism—this idea is fundamental.

Now, the world is as it were included in the divine Beatitude, or more precisely, it is as if included in Being which for its part is so to speak the 'external' dimension of Bliss or of Self; we say 'external' inasmuch as we place ourselves at the standpoint of the world, which is the human standpoint, since it goes without saying that there is no kind of 'exteriority' in the Infinite. That is why it is said in theology that God has created the world 'by goodness': 'love' and 'goodness', as also 'beauty', are so many aspects of Bliss; this last is identified with All-Possibility. That the world is 'contained' in the divine Bliss or Goodness means, in relation to suffering—even in hell—that the being always keeps the gift, positive in itself, of existence and that all suffering necessarily is limited in its nature and duration, God alone being absolute.

The subjective principle emanating from the divine Subject traverses the Universe like a ray in order to find its term in the multitude of *ego*s. The formal world is characterised by the 'exterior limits' of its contents, therefore by a kind of indefinite segmentation[1]: thus its 'subjectivity' will be multiple, whence the innumerable diversity of souls. Man marks, for the terrestrial world that is his, the limit of the 'creative ray'; man's sufficient cause is being this limit, that is to say, providing a stop, after the manner of an echo or a mirror, to the 'ray of exteriorisation' of the Self; thus the human state is a gate of exit—and the only gate for the terrestrial world—not merely out of this world or the formal cosmos, but even out of the immense and numberless objectivation that is universal Existence; since it is a total microcosm, a 'plenary' 'I',[2] the state of man is at the same time a door open towards the Self and immortality.[3]

*

[1] In the formless or supra-formal world, which is the realm of the angelic states, all things are perceived as subsisting 'in the interior' of the subject, differences among the angelic subjects being marked by their modes of perception.

[2] And not a partial 'I' such as is, for instance, an animal *ego*.

[3] Is there any immortality outside the Self? Yes and no. There is also

In one of his hymns to *Hari*, Shankarâchârya says: 'Lord, although I and Thou make but One, I belong to Thee, but not Thou to me, just as the waves belong to the sea, but not the sea to the waves.' And in another hymn, Shaṅkara expresses himself thus: 'That which is the ceasing of mental agitation and supreme peacefulness; that which is the lake *Manikarnikâ* and pilgrimage *par excellence*; that which is the primordial, most pure Ganges, the river of Knowledge; this it is which is Benares, inborn Wisdom, and it is this which I am.'

paradisal immortality, but the latter 'comes to an end'—'upwards'—in the final reintegration (the *mahâpralaya* of the Hindus, or end of a 'life of *Brahmâ*') of Existence in the Self; but this ending, precisely, is a 'more' and not a 'less', a 'fulfilling' *in divinis* and not an 'abolition'.

7

The Ternary Aspect
of the Human Microcosm

Human life unfolds on three planes simultaneously, or rather, the *ego* is subject to three centres of attraction to which it responds in different ways, according to its own nature or value. We live at the same time in the body, the head and the heart, so that we may sometimes ask ourselves where the genuine 'I' is situated; in fact, the *ego*, properly speaking, the empirical 'I', has its sensory seat in the brain, but it gravitates towards the body and tends to identify itself with it, while the heart is symbolically the seat of the Self, of which we may be conscious or ignorant, but which is our true existential, intellectual, and so universal centre. It is, in a sense, the old triad *anima*, *animus*, *Spiritus*, with the difference however that *anima*—the 'spouse' of *animus*—is rather the vegetative and animal psychic entity than the body itself; but there is no clear line of demarcation here, since the body cannot be dissociated from its sensations, which in fact constitute our lower and de-centralised *ego*, with its downward drag and dispersive tendency.

The brain is to the body what the heart is to brain and body taken together. The body and the brain are as it were projected into the current of forms; the heart is as it were immersed in the immutability of Being. Body and brain are so to speak the heart exteriorised; their bipolarisation is explained by the fact of their exteriorisation. The formal world being made up of dualities, the Intellect, once it has been projected by virtue of its 'fall' into material and psychic substances, is split into two poles, the one intellectual and the other existential; it is divided into intelligence and existence, into brain and body. In the Intellect, intelligence is existence, and inversely; distinction of aspects does not in itself imply a scission. Scission occurs only in the world of forms.

In other terms: the mind is the centre of the body, while the Intellect is simultaneously the centre of mind and body; but it is corporeal, of course, only in so far as it is central to the body, that is to say, in so far as it is heart. In fact mind and body both reflect the Intellect, or rather, mind and body 'are' the Intellect, by bipolarised reflection, in the flux of peripheral Existence; neither of the two could reflect the Intellect in a total fashion, their bipolarisation being in short the sign of their remoteness from their common source. It is thus that the reflection of the sun cannot exist without the water that receives it; water, like the body, is the receptacle of the ray, solar in the first case and intellectual in the second; it has itself a solar or luminous quality by its capacity of reverberation.

This projection of the Intellect into the existential periphery has, as its result, not only bipolarisation into mind and body, or into inner *ego* and outer *ego*, but also the opening of the mind, through the medium of the faculties of sensation and action, towards the material world in which the body is plunged. In saying mind, one says both intellectual centre and material periphery: the mind, while being of intellectual substance, is turned towards matter, towards the plane of crystallisation, segmentation and movement; it emanates from the Intellect and disperses itself in matter. As we have said, the mind is to the body what the Intellect is to mind and body taken together; this pair is Intellect bipolarised in relation to matter or more precisely to sensible or sensory Existence. The heart and the brain, far from producing respectively the Intellect and the mind, are only their traces in the body, traces necessary by virtue of its 'existential intellectuality'.

*

The fundamental reason for the scission in the 'externalised Intellect' is existential separation into 'subject' and 'object': whilst in the Intellect knowledge is being and being is knowledge, in peripheral Existence knowledge becomes mind and being becomes body, without it being possible however to say that the mind is 'non-existent' or that the body is 'non-conscious'; on the other hand this polarity is already prefigured in the Intellect, which itself also has an aspect of subject or 'knowing' and an aspect of object or 'being', and yet again an aspect of beatitude or 'joy'.[1] In the terrestrial creature this 'joy' becomes life, which unites the *ego*-subject, mind, with the *ego*-object, body; in the Intellect these aspects, though distinguishable, are not separated, any more than are form, luminosity and heat in the sun, although these aspects appear separate on earth and from the terrestrial point of view.

The Intellect, in a certain sense, is 'divine' for the mind and 'created' or 'manifested' for God: it is none the less necessary to distinguish between a 'created Intellect' and an 'uncreated Intellect', the latter being the divine Light and the former the reflection of this Light at the centre of Existence; 'essentially', they are One, but 'existentially', they are distinct, so that we could say, in Hindu style, that the Intellect is 'neither divine nor non-divine', an elliptical expression which doubtless is repugnant to the Latin and Western mentality, but which transmits an essential shade of meaning. However that may be, when we speak of the Heart-Intellect, we mean the universal faculty which has the human heart for its symbolical seat, but which, while being 'crystallised' according to different planes of reflection, is none the less 'divine' in its single essence.

Every manifestation or creature is distinguished from the Principle or the Creator by an inversion of relationships, comparable to that which is seen in every reflection[2]; the tree reflected in water is upside down, but it is still a tree, for the mirror changes relationships but not content.[3] Similarly Intellect as manifested must itself also be distinguished by an

[1] This is the Hindu *Trimurti*, the 'Triple Manifestation' of the universal Intellect (*Buddhî*): *Sat* (Being), *Chit* (Consciousness), *Ânanda* (Beatitude).

[2] It is the law of 'inverse analogy' presented by Guénon in *Man and his Becoming*. (Luzac.)

[3] All the same, to invert is to lie. The world, while being truth by its content, is 'lie' in respect of God. God alone is Truth.

inversion from its non-manifested or divine Prototype. In fact, whilst all is contained principially in the 'Self', the universal Intellect is on the contrary like the content as it were of the manifested Universe; it is the centre or the heart of the world, while the divine Intellect is neither centre nor periphery: it contains all without being periphery and it determines all without being centre; it 'is real' in 'knowing', and it 'knows' in 'being real'.[1]. The difference does not then concern the absoluteness of the Intellect, but solely its ontological 'situation': the manifested Intellect, without ceasing to be 'divine' in essence, is none the less subject to cosmic objectivation, and thereafter to an indefinite diversity of lesser objectivations.

We have just said that Intellect as such, whatever its metaphysical degree, is 'divine' in essence; consequently, what we have said of Intellect *in divinis*, namely that there is in it no polarisation, applies also to the universal Intellect, not indeed in so far as it is manifest, certainly, but in so far as, being Intellect, it has the nature of Intellect.

The fact that 'all is *Atmâ*'—and this must in no way be understood in a pantheistic sense, things 'being *Atmâ*' in so far as they are distinct from nothingness and also through their symbolism, but not 'in themselves'—this fact,[2] we say, is proved by the ambiguity of what lies at the apparent limit whether of the cosmos, or of the Principle. We have seen that the Intellect is ambiguous because, while being 'divine', it is also manifested, and the same applies to Being: whilst it is already 'relative', it is still divine. The 'line of demarcation' between God and the world can then be thought of in different ways, according to whether one is distinguishing between the ontological Principle and its creation, or between universal Intellect and things, or again between the Absolute and the relative, the Real and the unreal, the Self and its objectivations,

---

[1] We put 'to be real' in place of 'to be' in order to avoid the ontological restriction; in pure metaphysics, God is not limited to Being. He is supra-personal while still also being personal.

[2] The word 'fact' has here only a verbal function, for it is obvious that a principial reality is not a 'fact'.

Paramâtmâ and *Mâyâ*: in this last case, which metaphysically
is the most important and the 'most true', the 'personal God',
Being, is found on the 'hither side' of the 'demarcation line',
for He is already objectivised in relation to the absolute
Subject, the Self, or rather He is the principial objectivation,
that from which all others result, but without 'emanation'
since Being is Principle; Being is 'God', but also 'relativity' or
'lesser absoluteness' in relation to Beyond-Being.[1] On the other
hand, when one distinguishes between the personal and creating
God and the creation, the 'line' in question separates the ontological Principle from its manifestation, or Being from exist-
ences; it is then drawn 'below the line' separating Reality and
non-reality,[2] or the Absolute and the relative, or the Self and
'illusion'. Finally when we distinguish between Intellect and
the *ego*—the latter being mental and corporeal—the 'line of
demarcation' between 'Divine' and 'created' crosses the actual
'territory' of the created, and so is situated 'below' the preceding line. In other words, Being is 'ambiguous' because it is
at the same time absolute and relative, or because it is absolute
while being situated in relativity, or again, to express ourselves
more boldly though perhaps all the more suggestively, because
it is the 'relative Absolute'. In an analogous way, Intellect is
'ambiguous' because it is at the same time divine and human,
uncreated and created, principial and manifested, which can
never be said of Being; Intellect is 'manifested Principle', while
Being is 'Principle determined' or 'made relative', but always
non-manifested. The ambiguity of the 'partition' between the
two great orders of Reality presents itself as if, in one case,
manifestation 'encroached' on the Principle, whilst in the other
the Principle 'would encroach' on manifestation.

*

Looking at man from the outside, two units of form can be

[1] This is Eckhart's distinction between *Gott* (God) and *Gottheit*
(Godhead).
[2] Or 'lesser reality', according to the point of view.

distinguished, the body and the head, and it can be said that each alike manifests a third element which is hidden, namely the heart. The outer man is perfect to the extent that his face and body express the heart, not only by beauty, but also, and indeed above all, by interiorisation; this is what the sacred image of the Buddha translates by the immutable majesty of the face with half-closed eyes and also by the symmetry and calm of the pose and by the gesture indicating silence, cessation, return to the centre, contemplation: pre-eminently this is the image of the Heart-Intellect penetrating into the body, and absorbing it in its own infinitude. Spirituality is, in short, none other than the penetration of the mind-body by the Intellect, which as it were advances on it, fills it and transforms it with God as term; but it is also the return—not by 'projection' this time, but by 'absorption'—of the mind-body into the Intellect. It is this that enables one to understand that the fundamental yogic position—which the image of Buddha transposes onto the plane of sacramental art—derives from a veritable alchemy of forms and of centres. Sometimes, the Buddha is represented standing, and sometimes lying on one side[1]; he is contemplative in action (upright position) as in non-action (seated position); his sleep is wakefulness and his waking, sleep (lying position). Sapiential sanctity is the sleep of the *ego* and the waking of the Self or of the Void; the moving surface of our being must sleep, for: 'I sleep, but my heart waketh'. It is not disinterested activity which must sleep, but the life of the instincts, the passional comings and goings of the soul. Man's habitual dream lives in the past and in the future: the soul is as if suspended in the past and at the same time swept along by the future, instead of reposing presently in Being. God is 'Being' in the absolute sense, that is to say in so far as He is Essence and not determination or movement; He loves what is conformable to Being, so that in the soul it is the aspect 'being' which He loves above all; this aspect is not distinct from that of

[1] The Koran refers to the same symbolism when it teaches that God should be remembered 'upright, seated or lying on one side'.

'consciousness', and this amounts to saying that to return to our 'being' is to realise pure 'consciousness'. God loves our actions only in so far as they are expressions of our 'being' or ways towards it; our activity in itself is without importance.

The triad 'heart-brain-body'—or 'Intellect-mind-body'—is prefigured in the triad 'Self-Mind-World': just as the divine Mind—universal Intellect—and the macrocosm of which it is the luminous and celestial centre, constitute a bipolarised projection of the Self in 'existential nothingness', so too the mind and body that it illumines and directs project the Intellect into the existential periphery, which is the kingdom of alternatives; and just as the Self is 'absent' from manifestation as such, which covers it like a veil whilst of necessity also expressing it—for 'to exist' is 'to express'—so too the heart is hidden in man, while head and body—mind-intelligence and body-existence—are visible externally. The heart is to head and body what the Self is to the Spirit and to man. If 'the Word is made flesh', it is because the Heart-Intellect has penetrated into the night of the body in order to reintegrate 'projected' or 'separated' existence in the unity and peace of pure Being.

8

Love of God
Consciousness of the Real

It may sometimes seem that the sole element that can unite the soul to God is love, for love alone is desire of possession or of union, desire, the sublimation of which can engender the greatest sacrifices; while knowledge, seen from this angle, appears as a static element having no operative or unitive virtue. But to maintain this view is either a question of terminology—and in such a case 'knowledge' is taken to mean only theory, while there is no mode of spiritual union that 'love' is held to exclude—or it shows a misconception of metaphysical 'consciousness' which is an eminently concrete participation in the transcendent realities: far from denying love, or the fear which is its complement, this consciousness embraces them in surpassing them, and because it surpasses them.[1] Before being able to 'love', it is necessary to 'be conscious'; primarily it is light which the sun pours out, rather than heat, as is shown by the visibility of immeasurably distant stars; and to be conscious, in the sense which interests us here, is to fix the heart in the Real, in permanent 'remembering' of the Divine. Fear estranges

[1] 'The word "incantation" ... must be understood as referring essentially to an aspiration of the being towards the Universal with the object of obtaining an inner illumination, whatever may be the outward means ... that can be employed as accessory supports of the inward act, and which have as their effect the production of rhythmic vibrations causing a repercussion throughout the indefinite series of states of the being.' (René Guénon, *Man and his Becoming*, ch. XX. Luzac, 1945). 'And indeed many examples are to be met (with) in the *Veda* of persons who have neglected to carry out such rites ... or who have been prevented from doing so, and yet by maintaining their attention perpetually concentrated and fixed on the Supreme *Brahma* (in which consists the one and only really indispensable preparation), have acquired true Knowledge concerning It ...' (ibid., ch. XXII, p. 166; quotation from the *Brahma-Sutras*). In all this, it is indeed a matter of 'aspiration', of 'inner act' and of 'concentrated attention', but without there being a question of 'love' in the specific sense of the term.

from the world—love brings close to God; but consciousness 'is' already something of its content or its aim; it is true that this remark is also valid for other spiritual modes, but in a less direct way, since intellective consciousness alone surpasses human subjectivity by definition. In a certain sense, love saves because it includes the whole subject, while consciousness delivers because it excludes it.[1]

In the framework of gnosis, love has something impersonal about it, because the love of man for God is in a sense not to be separated from that of God for man. The divine quality of 'love' is everywhere, it is in the very substance of the Universe, 'created by love'; it belongs to no single person and embraces all; it derives in short from the supreme Beatitude, which is at the same time divine Contemplation and creative Will.

All men have the need, in some degree or another, to understand and to love; but there are men who understand only love and act through it alone, as there are others who are stirred only by sapiential consciousness; the element 'truth' then takes priority over the element 'life', if it can be so expressed. The fundamental contemplativity of these souls—and not the sharpness of their intelligence on lower planes—is equivalent to a need for total truth and cannot be halted by screens of form, any more than light can be halted in space; for these screens, being symbols, are transparent; only the blind believe them to be opaque. Contemplativity implies, further, a certain natural distance in respect of the world, not only because things appear in their metaphysical 'transparency'—external alternatives then lose much of their importance—but also because the human world is shown up in all its absurdity, so that the simple fact of enduring it is already an asceticism.

*

The fact that the term 'love' evokes above all the idea of

---

[1] This is not unrelated to the phonetic resemblance of the Latin words *amor* and *mors*. Love, which includes all, is a sort of death, and death, which excludes all, is like fainting from love.

sexual attraction and family affection indicates that it is not arbitrary to attribute to the way of love a character of emotiveness, even of sentimentalism, though this term is broadened, by the very force of things, once it becomes for an entire tradition the common denominator of all spirituality. It is precisely the idea of 'union'—comprised in the notion of love— which allows us to give the name 'love' to that something which attaches us to God in an effective way; whatever may be our motives, we 'love' the place where we wish to be, the object we want to possess, the state we wish to enjoy. In this sense, we can accept without hesitation the postulate of the pre-eminence of 'love' over a 'knowledge' that is still mental and inoperative.

Love thus stripped of its emotive aspect—but not of its character of 'union', without which the word would lose all meaning—is no other, in short, than the will: the latter obeys in fact intellectual as well as sentimental motives; it is neutral in itself, but never operates alone, its motive always coming from outside; but from another angle, the will lets itself get absorbed by what determines it and thus becomes as it were an aspect of the driving intention.

When Christ—in renewing the Law of Sinai which He came to 'fulfil' and not to 'destroy'—teaches the love of God[1] He distinguishes between 'heart', 'soul', 'strength' (Torah: 'might') and 'mind'; this 'love' excludes no faculty which unites with God and cannot thus be merely one term of an opposition, as when love and knowledge confront one another. If by the word 'love' the Torah and the Gospel express above all the idea of 'union', or of 'will for union', they make it clear, by the epithets that follow, that this comprises differing modes, in conformity with the diversity of man's nature; it would be necessary then to say, not, love alone draws towards God, but rather, what draws towards God is alone love.

*

Love, even when envisaged in its current sense and in its

[1] Deut. vi, 5, and x, 12; Matt. xxii, 37; Mark xii, 30; Luke x, 27.

psychological connotation, agrees readily with a desire to suffer for the Loved-one, since it burns to be able to prove its fullness.[1] Metaphysical consciousness, on the other hand, carries its dimensions within itself: the detachment which it implies is not really distinct from it, and that is why it imposes itself, not in so far as it can be a suffering or a sacrifice, but uniquely in so far as it is a 'void', a 'poverty' or an 'extinction' for the sake of plenitude of the Self.

There is all the same a mystical love which does not necessarily spill over into grief, and which, being contemplative rather than volitive, is akin to beauty; the condition of this love is a vision of the 'metaphysical transparency' of things, and so also, by compensation, a detachment in relation to them, which means that this love is close to gnosis. This connection between love and beauty—which appears pertinently in the realm of sex—allows the conception of a love which responds to the Beauty of God and of a Mercy which responds to the beauty of human virtues or, in a deeper sense, to the beauty of the divine virtues as reflected in man.[2] It is moreover the 'metaphysical transparency' of appearances which in principle permits the integration of pleasure into spirituality, even if only to the extent that this is inevitable. It is necessary to distinguish here between contingent level and absolute content, or between the aspect of 'manifestation' and that of 'revelation'; the first is animal or 'worldly' and the second spiritual. The demiurgic

---

[1] That is obvious in the case of women when one considers the pangs of child-birth; love of the creature for the Creator is of necessity a 'feminine' love, since we are passive in regard to what determines us.

[2] This mysticism of beauty is more oriental than western, and more contemplative than volitive; we find it in men like St. Bernard and St. Francis of Assisi, as also in Fra Angelico, not forgetting the troubadours and the *Fedeli d'Amore* with whom it seems to have given rise to an alchemy with erotic symbolism akin, perhaps, to certain tantric doctrines. Let us also mention, in relation to Judaeo-Christianity, the symbolism of the *Song of Songs*, and in a much more general sense the function at once aesthetic and spiritual of the liturgy. In Islam, 'the Beautiful' (*El-Jamîl*) is a divine Name, and the virtues are sometimes called 'beauties' (*husnâ*).

tendency moves away from God—from the macrocosmic point of view—but with a creative and revelatory intention, and this second characteristic allows the microcosm to return to God through the medium of the symbol; the satanic tendency, on ·the contrary, separates from God, and so is opposed to Him; however, the very least of insects is obedient to Heaven, by its subjection to natural laws as much as by its form. The devil's greatest vexation is that he is obliged to be a symbol of God, an inverted symbol, doubtless, but always recognisably and ineffaceably a symbol.

*

The consciousness of which we have spoken has as it were two faces, one turned towards the Absolute and the other towards relativities. Just as it is impossible to love God without loving one's neighbour too and without hating the world and the *ego*, so too consciousness of the Self and of its primary objectivations demands and brings with it consciousness of the cosmic structures, whether of the macrocosm or of the microcosm.

To be conscious of the Self is to know, first of all—and we cannot set down what words cannot contain—that we are not really ourselves except beyond the limit of our empirical *ego*; to know that this *ego* is foreign to our innermost reality—a reality which does not belong to us, but to which we belong—although the *ego* reflects this reality in its own way and at its own level; it is to know also, and correlatively, that God is All-Reality, that the world is 'nothing'—otherwise it would be infinite and eternal—and that we ourselves are 'nothing' in relation to our first Cause; that the world is in God, but that God is not of this world.

In the cosmic order, consciousness necessarily approaches the perspectives of fear and of love, for the simple reason that the situation of our *ego* in the Universe could not appear to us as something 'neutral'. To be conscious of death and of the Judgement is to approach, whether one likes it or not, a 'wisdom of fear'; for the individual as such cannot like dying, unless to escape evils that appear even greater, and above all, he cannot remain indifferent to the idea of the beyond, given that 'God alone is good' and that there is, in principle, little chance that the generality of ordinary mortals will have nothing to fear from the divine 'Hand of Rigour'. In an analogous though different sense—and there is no analogy without difference—to be conscious of the divine Mercy is to enter into the universal ray of love; for by the force of things it is to turn towards God with hope and joy; so too with consciousness of the Real Presence of the Divine, into which we 'emerge' from space and time, to find there again the pure essence of all we can love here below.

9

Seeing God Everywhere

One often hears it said that it is necessary to 'see God every-where' or 'in everything'. For men who believe in God this does not seem a difficult conception; nevertheless there are many degrees involved, extending from simple reverie to intellectual intuition. How can one attempt to 'see God', who is invisible and infinite, in what is visible and finite without the risk of deluding oneself or falling into error, or without giving the idea a meaning so vague that the words lose all significance? That is the question we propose to clarify here, though this means returning to certain points we have already treated elsewhere.

First of all, we must consider in the things around us—and also in our own soul in so far as it is an object of our intelligence—the something that might be called the 'miracle of existence'. Existence implies miracle: it is by miracle that things are, so to speak, separated from nothingness; the gap between them and nothingness is infinite, and seen from this angle the least speck of dust possesses something of the absolute, of the 'divine'. To say that one must see God everywhere means, above all, that one must see Him in the existence of beings and of things, our own included.

But phenomena do not possess existence alone, for otherwise they would not be distinct; they also possess qualities which are as it were superimposed on existence and deploy its virtualities. The quality which distinguishes a good thing from a bad resembles, though on a lesser scale, the existence which distinguishes each thing from nothingness[1]; in consequence

---

[1] We speak here of nothingness as if it had some reality, which is metaphysically necessary in certain cases, although logically absurd. If there is no nothingness, there is nevertheless a 'principle of nothing-ness', a principle which—since nothingness does not exist—always stops halfway. This principle is like the inverse shadow of the infinitude of Beyond-Being; it is *Mâyâ* which is illusorily detached from *Atmâ*, though not able to emerge from *Atmâ*, still less to abolish *Atmâ*.

positive qualities represent God, as does pure and simple existence. Beings are attracted by qualities, because they are attracted by God; every quality or virtue, whether it be the slightest of physical properties or the most profound of human virtues, transmits to us something of the divine Perfection, which is its immutable source, so that, metaphysically speaking, we could have no motive for love other than this Perfection.

But there is yet another 'dimension' to be considered by the man who seeks the remembrance of God in things. The enjoyment that qualities afford us shows us that these latter not only exist around us, but also concern us personally through Providence; for a landscape which exists out of our sight is one thing, and a landscape we can see is another. There is then a 'subjective-temporal' dimension which is, so to say, added to the 'objective-spatial' dimension; things recall God to us, not only in so far as they are good or display an aspect of goodness, but also in so far as we can perceive this goodness or can enjoy it in a still more direct way. In the air we breathe, and which might be denied us, we meet God in the sense that the divine Giver is in the gift. This manner of 'seeing God' in his gifts corresponds to 'thanksgiving', while the perception of qualities corresponds to 'praise'; as for the 'vision' of God in mere existence, this gives birth in the soul to a general or fundamental consciousness of the divine Reality.

Thus, God reveals himself not only by the existence and by the qualities of things, but by the gift He makes of them to us; He reveals himself also by the contraries, namely by the limitation of things and by their defects,[1] and again by the absence or disappearance of something which, being good, is useful and agreeable to us. It will be noticed that the concrete opposite of existence is not nothingness—the latter is only an abstraction—but limitation, the limitation which prevents existence from extending to pure Being, from becoming God . . . . Things are limited in very many ways, but above all by their existential

---

[1] It is in this sense that Meister Eckhart could say: 'The more he blasphemes, the more he praises God.'

determinations, which, on the terrestrial level, are matter, form, number, space, time. A clear distinction must be made between the aspect of 'limit' and the aspect of 'defect'; in fact, the ugliness of a creature is not of the same order as the spatial limitation of a perfect body, for the latter expresses a form, a normative principle or a symbol, while the former corresponds only to a lack and merely confuses the clarity of the symbolism. However that may be, what God reveals by the limitation of things, by their defects and also, in relation to the human subject, by the privation of things or of qualities, is the 'non-divine', hence 'illusory' or 'unreal' character of all that is not He.

*

All things are only the accidentalities of a unique and universal substance, Existence, which remains always virgin in relation to its products; it manifests, but is not itself manifested; that is to say it is the divine act, the creative act which, starting from Being, produces the totality of creatures. It is Existence that is real, not things; substance, not its accidents; the unvarying, not the variations. Since this is so, how would things not be limited, and how would they not proclaim, by their multiple limitations, the unicity of the divine Word, and thereby of God? For universal Substance is none other than the creative Word, the word 'Let there be!' from which all things spring.

To say 'exist' is to say 'to have qualities', but it is also to say ' to have limitations', even defects. We have already noted that things are limited, not only in themselves, but also in relation to us; they are limited and ephemeral, and at the same time they escape us, whether by their remoteness in space, or by the destiny that carries them away. This again allows us to 'see God in everything', for if God manifests His Reality, His Plenitude and His Presence in His act of giving, He manifests our relativity, our emptiness, our absence—in relation to Him—in removing, that is to say, in taking back what He had given.

Just as qualities express existence on the actual level of the latter, so too limitations express, in an inverse sense, the metaphysical unreality of things. Here lies a new manner of 'seeing God everywhere': for each thing, in existing, is by that very fact 'unreal' in relation to absolute Reality; we should therefore discern in all things not only the aspects of existence, but also the 'nothingness' of the world before God, or, in other terms, its metaphysical unreality. And it is existence[1] itself which furnishes us with the 'substance' of this 'nothingness'; things are unreal or illusory to the exact extent that they are embedded in existence and that their contact with the divine Spirit thereby becomes more and more indirect.

Quality, we have said, expresses existence on the level of the latter itself; and we could say, analogously, that defect expresses limitation in a manner which is solely negative and accidental. For limitation maintains itself as it were between existence and nothingness: it is positive in so far as it delineates a form-symbol, and negative in so far as it disfigures this form in seeking to bring it back, as it were, towards the indistinction of the essence, but 'from below'; this is the classical confusion between the supra-formal and the non-formal, a confusion which, let it be said in passing, is the key to the art-forms called 'abstract' or 'surrealist'. However, although form has a positive function thanks to its power of expression, it limits at the same time that which it expresses, and which is an essence: the most beautiful body is like a congealed fragment of an ocean of inexpressible blessedness.

*

To all these categories of existence, subjective as well as objective, we can add those of symbolism. Although every phenomenon is of necessity a symbol, since existence is essentially expression or reflection, we must nevertheless distinguish degrees of content and of intelligibility: for example, there is a

[1] Existence is positive and 'divine' in relation to existing things and in so far as it is cause, but it is limitative and 'demiurgic' in relation to God, who, in the act of creating, limits Himself in a certain illusory sense, if such an expression is allowable; we say, an illusory sense, since God is immutable, impassible, inalterable.

difference that is one of degree—and not simply quantitative—between a direct symbol such as the sun and an indirect, quasi-accidental symbol; further, there is the negative symbol, the intelligibility of which may be perfect, but its content obscure; nor should we forget the double meaning of many symbols, though not of those that are most direct. The science of symbols —not simply a knowledge of traditional symbols—proceeds from the qualitative significances of substances, forms, spatial directions, numbers, natural phenomena, positions, relationships, movements, colours and other properties or states of things; we are not dealing here with subjective appreciations, for the cosmic qualities are ordered both in relation to Being and according to a hierarchy which is more real than the individual; they are, then, independent of our tastes, or rather they determine them to the extent that we are ourselves conformable to Being; we assent to the qualities to the extent that we ourselves are 'qualitative'.[1] Symbolism, whether it resides in nature or whether it is affirmed in sacred art, also corresponds to a manner of 'seeing God everywhere', on condition that this vision is spontaneous thanks to an intimate knowledge of the principles from which the science of symbols proceeds; this science coincides at a certain point with the 'discerning of spirits' which it transposes on to the plane of forms or phenomena, whence its close connection with religious art.

Now, 'how' do things symbolise God or 'divine aspects'? One cannot say that God is this tree, nor that this tree is God, but one can say that the tree is, in a certain respect, not 'other than God', or that, not being non-existent, it cannot not be God in any fashion. For the tree has firstly existence, then the life

[1] A man must be quite perverse to see no qualitative and objective difference between what is noble and what is mean, unless he takes his stand at the transcendent point of view of the non-differentiation of *Atmâ*, which is an absolutely different thing from a subversive and iconoclastic egalitarianism. However that may be, it is this science of qualitative phenomena which allows the aberrations of contemporary art to be 'placed' inexorably and the veil of its false mystery to be torn aside.

which distinguishes it from minerals, then its particular qualities which distinguish it from other plants, and finally its symbolism; all of these are for the tree so many manners, not only of 'not being nothingness', but also of affirming God in one or another respect: life, creation, majesty, axial immobility or generosity.—We say, 'not being nothingness': but in a certain sense, God alone is 'that which is not nothing'; He alone is 'non-non-existence'—two negatives at once, but having their precise function. Truths of this kind can give rise, indirectly and by deviation, to pantheism and idolatry, but that does not prevent them from being true and therefore, to say the least, legitimate on their own level.

Symbolism would have no meaning if it were not a contingent, but always conscious, mode of perception of Unity; for 'to see God everywhere', is to perceive above all the Unity—*Atmâ*, the Self—in phenomena. According to the *Bhagavad-Gitâ*, the cognition which recognises in all beings an essence unique, imperishable, indivisible, although diffused in separate objects, proceeds from *Sattwa* (the tendency that is 'luminous', 'ascendent', 'conformable to Being', *Sat*); and the same text continues: 'But the cognition which, led astray by the multiplicity of objects, sees in all beings diverse and distinct entities, proceeds from *rajas* (the "fiery", "expansive" tendency). As for the shuttered cognition which, without going back to causes is attached to a particular object as if that were all in all, this proceeds from *tamas* (the "dark" and "downwards" tendency).' (xviii, 20–22.) It is necessary here to take into account the angle from which things are envisaged: the cosmic tendencies (*gunas*) are not only in the mind of man, they clearly enter also into his faculties of relative knowledge and the realms corresponding to them, so that reason can no more escape diversity than can the eye; further, to say that such and such a cognition 'recognises an unique essence in all beings', amounts to affirming that these beings exist on their own plane. It is a question then of admitting not that there are no objective differences around us, but that the latter are in no way opposed to the perception of the unity of the essence; the 'passional' perspective (*rajas*) is at fault, not because it perceives differences, but because it lends them an absolute character, as if each being were a separate existence; so also does the eye in a certain way, precisely because it corresponds existentially to a 'passional' view in so far as it belongs to the *ego* which is 'made of passion'. The Intellect, which perceives the unity of essence in things, discerns at the same time the differences of modes and of degrees in function of this unity, apart from which any distinguishing between the *gunas* would be excluded.

*

We referred above to the conditions of sensory or psycho-physical existence; space, time, form, number, substance—modes which moreover are not all reducible to our plane of existence (since the latter could not be a closed system), any more than they enclose man wholly, since man has extension towards the Infinite. These conditions denote so many principles which allow one to 'see God in things'; space gives extension and conserves, while limiting by form; time limits and devours, while giving extension by duration; form both expresses and limits at the same time; number is a principle of expansion, but without the force of quality, or, it could be said, the virtue of form; and finally substance, which on the physical plane becomes 'matter'[1], denotes existence on such and such a level, hence the 'level of existence'.[2] Form, in itself qualitative, has something quantitative about it when it is material; number, in itself quantitative, has something qualitative when it is abstract. The materiality of form adds size

[1] This fifth condition has sometimes been called 'life', doubtless to express the idea that inertia could not be absolute, or that the ether possesses a certain potentiality of life, without which life—'breath' (πνεῦμα or *prâna*)—would find no receptacle.

[2] The Sanskrit word for 'matter', *bhûta*, includes a meaning of 'substance' or of 'subsistence'; matter derives from substance, it is a reflection of it on the plane of 'gross' coagulations, and is connected, through substance, with Being.

and so quantity to the latter; the symbolic character of number delivers it from its quantitative function and confers on it a principial value, hence a quality.[1] Time, which is 'vertical' in relation to space which is 'horizontal' (although a geometrical symbolism is barely proper to a consideration which clearly goes outside the spatial condition) exceeds the limits of terrestrial existence and is projected in a certain fashion and within certain bounds into the 'beyond', a fact of which the connection in terrestrial life between psychic life and time already offers a foretaste; this connection is more intimate than that which links the soul with the space surrounding us, as is shown by the fact that it is easier to abstract oneself, in concentration, from spatial extension than from duration; the soul of a blind man is as it were cut off from space, but not from time.

As for matter, it is, still more directly than the subtle or soul substance, universal substance 'congealed'[2] or 'crystallised' by the cold proximity of 'nothingness'; this 'nothingness' the process of manifestation could never reach, for the simple reason that absolute 'nothingness' does not exist, or rather that it exists only by way of 'indication', 'direction' or 'tendency' in the work of creation itself; an image of this is seen in the fact that cold is only a privation and thus has no positive reality,

[1] This is number in the Pythagorean sense, of which the universal rather than the quantitative import is already to be divined in geometrical figures; the triangle and the square are 'personalities' and not quantities, they are essentials and not accidentals. Whilst one obtains ordinary number by addition, qualitative number results, on the contrary, from an internal or intrinsic differentiation of principial unity; it is not added to anything and does not depart from unity. Geometrical figures are so many images of unity; they exclude one another, or rather, they denote different principial qualities; the triangle is harmony, the square, stability; these are 'concentric' not 'serial' numbers.

[2] This 'congealing' does not reach substance itself, any more than, in the order of the five elements, 'solidification'—or the diversification of the elements in general—reaches the ether which subsists in them. All the same this comparison is not adequate, since the ether is an element and is not then situated on another plane, despite its 'central' position and its 'virginity', whilst universal substance is transcendent in relation to its productions.

though it transforms water into snow and ice, as if it had the power to produce bodies.

Space 'sets out' from the point or the centre; it is 'expansion' and it 'tends' towards infinitude, without ever being able to attain it; time sets out from the instant or the present[1]; it is duration and it tends towards eternity; form sets out from simplicity; it is differentiation or complexity and it tends towards perfection; number sets out from unity; it is multiplicity or quantity and it tends towards totality[2]; finally matter sets out from ether; it is crystallization or density and it tends towards immutability, which is at the same time indestructibility. In each of these cases, the 'middle term'—what the respective condition 'is'—seeks in short the perfection or virtue of the 'point of departure', but it seeks it on its own level or rather in its own movement, where it is impossible that it should be attained: if expansion had the virtue of the point it would be infinity; if duration had the virtue of the instant, it would be eternity; if form had the virtue of simplicity, it would be perfection; if number had the virtue of unity, it would be totality; if matter had the virtue—immutable because omnipresent—of ether, it would be immutability.

If it be objected that, on the formal plane, perfection is

---

[1] In relation to the 'point' and the 'instant', the 'centre' and the 'present' denote a perspective at once qualitative and subjective; qualitative subjectivity, because the subject is the Self. The objective terms—'point' and 'instant'—certainly imply this same 'quality', but the spiritual relationship—not the metaphysical relationship—is less direct and less apparent, precisely because the respective notions are detached from life.

[2] In these two conditions, form and number, the respective points of departure—simplicity and unity—have a concrete existence, doubtless because these conditions are 'contents' in relation to space and time, which are 'containers'; on the other hand, the points of departure of these latter conditions—the point and the instant—have respectively neither extent nor duration. None the less, spherical simplicity is not one form amongst others, since it is incomparable, any more than unity is a quantity properly speaking, since it is not added to anything; if there were only simplicity and unity there would be neither form nor number.

attained by the sphere, we reply that formal perfection could not be restricted to the simplest form, for what distinguishes a beautiful form of complex character—such as the human body for example—from the sphere, is in no way a lack of perfection, the less so since the formal principle tends precisely towards complexity; it is only therein that it can realise beauty. But this in no way signifies that perfection could be attained on this plane; in fact, complex perfection would demand a form which would combine the most rigorous necessity or intelligibility with the greatest diversity, and this is impossible because formal possibilities are innumerable to the extent that they get further, by way of differentiation, from the initial spherical form. In engulfing oneself in complexity, one can attain the 'unilateral' or 'relatively absolute' perfection of a given beauty, certainly, but not the integral and absolute perfection of all beauty; the condition of pure necessity is realised only in the spherical and 'undifferentiated' protoform.

What enters into space, enters also into time; what enters into form, enters also into number; what enters into matter, thereby enters into form, number, space, time. Space, which 'contains' like a matrix and which 'preserves', recalls Goodness or Mercy to us; it is for us like a 'matrix of immortality', death being birth into eternal Life; space conserves and is connected with love; time, on the contrary, ceaselessly throws us into a 'past' which is no more and carries us towards a 'future' which is not yet, or rather will never be, and which we do not know, save for death, the sole certitude of life; this implies that time is associated with Rigour or Justice and that it is connected with fear. As for matter, it recalls Reality to us, for it is that mode of 'non-non-existence' which is everywhere apparent to us, in our body just as when we see the Milky Way; form reminds us of the divine Law or the universal norm, for it is either veridical or erroneous, exact or false, essential or accidental; finally, number unfolds before us the limitlessness of All-Possibility, which like the sand of the desert or the stars of the sky is not to be numbered.

It is in vain that space would limit its contents, it cannot prevent them from existing; and it is in vain that time would prolong its contents, they will one day cease to exist just the same. Duration does not abolish ephemerality any more than spatial limitation abolishes extension. In space, nothing is ever wholly lost; in time, all is lost without remedy.

Existence is manifested *a priori* by substance. The latter has two containers, space and time, of which the first is positive and the second negative; it has also two modes, form and number, of which the first is limitative and the second expansive. Number reflects space, since it extends; form reflects time, since it restricts.

If man could live a thousand years, he would doubtless end by feeling himself crushed by the limits of things, hence also by space, time, form, number, matter; by compensation, he would see in contents only essences. A child or indeed an ordinary man sees, on the contrary, only contents, without essences and without limits.

*

These conditions of our existence on earth have, each one of them, two 'openings' towards God: space implies, on the one hand, the geometric point or the 'centre' and, on the other, limitless extension, the 'infinite'; likewise time implies the instant or the 'present', as well as indefinite duration, 'eternity'; in space we are as it were between the centre and the infinite, and in time, between the present and eternity, and these are then so many dwellings of God which take us out of the two 'dimensions of existence'; we cannot prevent ourselves from thinking of them when we are conscious of these conditions in which we live and which so to speak live in us. The centre and the infinite, the present and eternity, are respectively the poles of the conditions of space and time, but equally we escape these conditions by these very poles: the centre is no longer in space, strictly speaking, any more than the geometric point has extension, and the absolute present or the pure instant is no longer in duration: as for the infinite, it is in a way 'non-space', as eternity is 'non-time'.

Again let us consider the condition, form; in form there lie geometric perfection and bodily perfection, and both reveal God; the Creator manifests himself in the 'absoluteness' of the circle, the square, the cross, as in the beauty—the 'infinity'—of man or of a flower; geometrical beauty is 'cold', bodily beauty 'warm'. But strictly speaking, the 'centre' of the formal condition is the void; elementary geometrical forms, starting with the sphere, are only the first 'issuings' of form out of the void, being then at the same time the first 'expressions' and 'negations' of the latter. The sphere is the form which remains nearest the void, whence its perfection of simplicity; the human body, in its normative beauty—and the varied modes which it comprises —is what approaches most nearly to plenitude, corresponding to the opposite perfection, that of complexity. Plenitude is that which brings together a maximum of homogeneous aspects, or which introduces totality into form: the sphere and man correspond, in formal mode, to unity and totality; what number expresses in abstract, separative and quantitative mode, form expresses in concrete, unitive and qualitative mode. Zero is to unity as the void is to the sphere; unity denotes God, while totality is equivalent to His manifestation, the cosmos.

*

'To see God everywhere', is to see Oneself (*Atmâ*) in everything; it is to be conscious of the analogical correspondences—in so far as they are 'modes of identity'—between the principles or possibilities which, included first in the divine Nature, spread out or reverberate 'towards nothingness' and constitute the microcosm as well as the macrocosm, of which they create at the same time the receptacles and the contents. Space and time are receptacles; form and number appear as contents, although they are containers in relation to the substances which they coagulate or which they segment. Matter is, in a more visible way, both container and content at the same time;

it 'contains' things and it 'fills' space, its contents are gnawed
and devoured by time, but itself it remains quasi non-temporal,
to the extent that it coincides with the whole of duration.

The problem of time is intimately linked with that of the
soul and can give rise to the following question: what meaning
must be given to the dogmatic doctrine of the soul held by
Monotheists, according to which the soul would have no end,
while having had a beginning? The metaphysical absurdity of
an eternity created in time, or of a purely 'unilateral' perpetuity, is evident; but since theological orthodoxy excludes
pure and simple absurdity, one must seek beyond the words
and in symbolism for the explanation of a doctrine so contradictory. Let us say at once that Monotheism includes in its
perspective only what directly interests man, so that it appears
as a 'spiritual nationalism' of the human race; but, since the
state preceding our birth on earth was as little human as are
the animal or angelic states, it is treated as non-existent,
exactly as are the souls of animals and of plants; hence, we are
called 'soul' only from the moment of our human birth, or
rather from the mother's womb. But there is something else of
much more importance; the creation of the soul in time—that
is to say its entry into the human state—expresses our relativity;
by contrast, the celestial perpetuity of the soul, or its eternity
with God, concerns its absolute side, the 'uncreated' quality of
its essence; we are relative and absolute at the same time, and
this fundamental paradox of our being explains what the
theological doctrine of the soul may have of illogical or
'mysterious' in its very formulation. It must not be forgotten,
on the other hand, that *creatio ex nihilo* affirms, above all, a
divine causality in the face of an ever threatening 'naturalism';
and to say that the soul is 'eternal' can only mean, on the level
of absolute truth, that it is 'essentially' the Self.

*

The faculty of 'seeing God in everything' can be independent
of all intellectual analysis, it can be a grace, the modes of which

are imponderables and which springs from a profound love of God. When we say 'intellectual analysis', we do not mean speculations in the void: the 'categories' of which we have spoken are by no means 'abstract', but their perception evidently depends on a discernment which appears to be abstract from the point of view of sensations and which, though far from delighting in sterile dissections, is nevertheless obliged to 'separate' in order to 'unite'. Separation and union alike are both in the nature of things, each, it might be said, on its own level; the eye, the better to see a mountain, needs a certain distance; this distance reveals differences; it permits visual analysis, but, at the same time, it 'unites' or synthesises in furnishing the adequate and total image of the mountain.

To see God everywhere and in everything, is to see infinity in things, whereas human animality sees only their surface and their relativity; and it is to see at the same time the relativity of the categories in which man moves, believing them to be absolute. To see the infinite in the finite is to see that this flower before us is eternal, because an eternal spring is declared through its fragile smile; to see relativity is to grasp that this instant that we are living is not 'now', that it 'is past' even before it has arrived, and that, if time could be stopped, with all beings remaining fixed as in a river of ice, the human masquerade would appear in all its sinister unreality; all would seem absurd, save only the 'remembrance of God' which is situated in the immutable.

To see God everywhere is essentially this: to see that we are not, that He alone is. If, from a certain angle, humility can be called the greatest of the virtues this is because it implies in the last analysis the cessation of egoity, and for no other reason. With a small change of viewpoint one could say as much of each fundamental virtue: perfect charity is to lose oneself for God, for one cannot be lost in God without giving oneself, in addition, to men. If love of one's neighbour is capital, on the strictly human plane, it is not only because the 'neighbour' is in the final analysis 'Self' as are 'we', but also because this human

charity—or this projection into the 'other'—is the sole means
possible, for the majority of men, of being detached from the
'I'; it is less difficult to project the *ego* into 'the other' than to
lose it for God, although the two things are indissolubly
linked.

*

Our form, is the *ego*: it is this mysterious incapacity to be
other than oneself, and at the same time the incapacity to be
entirely oneself and not 'other-than-Self'. But our Reality does
not leave us the choice and obliges us to 'become what we are',
or to remain what we are not. The *ego* is, empirically, a dream in
which we ourselves dream ourselves; the contents of this dream,
drawn from our surroundings, are at bottom only pretexts, for
the *ego* desires only its own life: whatever we may dream, our
dream is always only a symbol for the *ego* which wishes to
affirm itself, a mirror that we hold before the 'I' and which
reverberates its life in multiple fashions. This dream has
become our second nature; it is woven of images and of
tendencies, static and dynamic elements in innumerable
combinations: the images come from outside and are integrated
into our substance; the tendencies are our responses to the
world around us; as we exteriorise ourselves, we create a world
in the image of our dream, and the dream thus objectivised
flows back upon us, and so on and on, until we are enclosed in a
tissue, sometimes inextricable, of dreams exteriorised or
materialised and of materialisations interiorised. The *ego* is like
a watermill whose wheel, under the drive of a current—the
world and life—turns and repeats itself untiringly, in a series
of images always different and always similar.

The world is as if the 'conscious Substance' which is the Self
had fallen into a state which would cut it up in many different
ways and would inflict on it endless accidents and infirmities;
and in fact, the *ego* is ignorance floundering in objective modes
of ignorance, such as time and space. What is time, if not
ignorance of what will be 'after', and what is space, if not

ignorance of what escapes our senses? If we were 'pure consciousness' like the Self, we would be 'always' and 'everywhere';
that is to say we would not be 'I', for that, in its empirical
actuality, is entirely a creation of space and time. The *ego* is
ignorance of what is 'the other'; our whole existence is woven
of ignorances; we are like the Self frozen, then hurled to earth
and split into a thousand fragments; we observe the limits
which surround us, and we conclude that we are fragments of
consciousness and of being. Matter grips us like a kind of
paralysis, it imposes on us the heaviness of a mineral, and
exposes us to the miseries of impurity and of mortality; form
shapes us according to such and such a model, it imposes on us
such and such a mask and cuts us off from a whole to which we
are none the less tied, though at death it lets us fall as a tree lets
fall its fruit; finally, number is what repeats us—inside ourselves as also around us—and what, in repeating us, diversifies
us, for two things can never be absolutely identical; number
repeats form as if by magic, and form diversifies number and
must thus create itself ever anew, because the All-Possibility
is infinite and must manifest its infinitude. But the *ego* is not
only multiple externally, in the diversity of souls, it is also
divided within itself, in the diversity of tendencies and of
thoughts, which is not the least of our miseries; for 'strait is the
gate' and 'a rich man shall hardly enter into the kingdom of
heaven'.

And since we are 'not other' than the Self, we are condemned
to eternity. Eternity lies in wait for us, and that is why we must
find again the Centre, that place where eternity is blessedness.
Hell is the reply to the rim which makes itself Centre, or to
the multitude that usurps the glory of Unity; it is the reply of
Reality to the *ego* wanting to be absolute, and condemned so to
be without power so to be. . . . The Centre is the Self 'freed', or
rather that which has never ceased to be free—eternally free.

THE CHRISTIAN TRADITION

10

The Christian Tradition
Some Thoughts on its Nature

In the perspective of gnosis, Christ, 'Light of the world', is the universal Intellect, as the Word is the 'Wisdom of the Father'. Christ is the Intellect of microcosms as well as that of the macrocosm, He is then the Intellect in us[1] as well as the Intellect in the Universe and *a fortiori* in God; in this sense, it can be said that there is no truth nor wisdom that does not come from Christ, and this is evidently independent of all consideration of time and place.[2] Just as 'the Light shineth in darkness; and the darkness comprehended it not', so too the Intellect shines in the darkness of passions and illusions. The relationship of the 'Son' to the 'Father' is analogous to the relationship of pure Love to Being or of the Intellect to the 'Self', and that is why we are, in the Intellect or in sanctifying Grace, 'brothers' of Christ.

Likewise Christ is prefigured in the whole of creation; this too has one aspect of incarnation and another of crucifixion. On a lesser scale, humanity, and with it the individual human, is an image of Christ, and comprises both aspects: man is

[1] 'The Word was the true Light, which lighteth every man . . .' (John i, 9).

[2] 'Now faith, says St. Paul, is the substance ("assurance" R.V.) of things hoped for, the evidence ("proving" R.V.) of things not seen. . . . Through faith we understand that the worlds were framed by the word of God, so that things which are seen were not made of things which do appear' (Heb. xi, 1, 3), which proves that faith is, to say the least, not contrary to gnosis; doubtless not all faith is metaphysical knowledge, but all metaphysical knowledge being an 'evidence of things not seen', is of the domain of faith. Gnosis is the perfection of faith in the sense that it combines this knowledge with the corresponding realisation; it is wisdom and sanctity: sanctifying wisdom and sapiential sanctity. The most external expression of the element 'realisation' is works, which on the one hand prove and on the other give life to faith, and without which it is 'dead, being alone' ('dead in itself' R.V.) (James ii, 17).

'incarnation' by his Intellect and his freedom, and 'crucifixion' by his miseries.

*

From the doctrinal point of view, Christian gnosis is nothing other than trinitarian metaphysics,[1] with their microcosmic application: our pure existence corresponds to the Father, our pure intelligence to the Son, and our pure will to the Holy Spirit. The vertical line of the cross denotes the relationship of the Father to the Son, while the horizontal line symbolises the Holy Spirit; the latter 'proceeds from the Father and is delegated by the Son', which signifies that the Spirit, which is at once Beatitude and Will, proceeds from the Father, then also from the Son (*Filioque*) in so far as He represents the Father, but not in so far as He is distinct from Him. The Father is Beyond-Being, the Son is Being and the Spirit is Beatitude and Manifestation; when the perspective is limited to ontology, the Father is Being, as such, and the Son the 'Consciousness' of Being. To say that the Spirit is Beatitude and Manifestation—whatever be the level of the perspective, ontological or supra-ontological—means that it is at once the 'inner life' and the 'creative projection' of Divinity; it is then an 'expansion' or a 'spiration' *in divinis* at the same time as a 'springing forth' *ex divinis*; it is, on the one hand, 'internal' or 'contemplative' Beatitude, and on the other 'external' or 'active' Beatitude. That is why in the sign of the cross the Holy Spirit 'occupies' the whole of the horizontal line; it could even be said that, in the making of this sign, the words '*Spiritus Sanctus*' designate the Spirit *in divinis*, and the word *Amen* the Spirit 'in creation', if such an expression can be allowed.

The Spirit 'as creation' is none other than the Virgin in three aspects, macrocosmic, microcosmic and historical: first it is Universal Substance, then it is the soul in a state of sanctifying

[1] Analogously, the metaphysics of Islam are unitary in the sense that they proceed by principial reductions to Unity, while the metaphysics of Judaism are at once unitary and denary. (*Decalogue, Sephiroth.*)

grace, and finally it is the human manifestation of these aspects, the Virgin Mary. In this sense, it can be said that the word *Amen* is a name of the Virgin, perfect creature—or perfect creation—and that, if the vertical line of the sign of the cross denotes the relationship of the Father and the Son, the horizontal line will denote the relationship of Husband and Spouse. The whole soul of the Virgin is one great *Amen*; there is nothing in it which is not an acquiescence in the Will of God.

*

Christian art comprises essentially three images: the Virgin and Child, the Crucifixion, the Holy Visage: the first image relates to the Incarnation, the second to the Redemption and the third to the Divinity of Christ. Man recapitulates these three symbols or mysteries respectively by purity which is the vehicle of 'Christ in us', by death to the world, and by sanctity or wisdom.

Strictly speaking, art forms part of the liturgy—in the broadest sense—for it is, like the latter, 'public work' ($\lambda\epsilon\iota\tau\upsilon\rho\gamma\iota\alpha$)[1]; hence, it cannot be abandoned to what is arbitrary in man. Art, like the liturgy properly so-called, constitutes the terrestrial 'garment' of God; it both envelops and unveils the divine Presence on earth.[2]

*

[1] According to St. Augustine, the liturgy is essentially simple, so that this simplicity is almost a criterion of authenticity; if it were otherwise, says the Bishop of Hippo, the liturgy would be lower than the Jewish Law which, after all, was given by God and not by the liturgists; further, he stresses the fact that Christian feasts are few in number.

[2] We have had occasion at various times to underline the sacred, hence immutable character of religious art: it is not a purely human thing, and above all, it does not consist in seeking impossible mysteries in non-existent profundities, as is the intention of modern art, which, instead of adapting 'our times' to truth, aims at adapting truth to 'our times'. In the context of artistic or artisan, and so of 'liturgic' expression, the terms 'Christian' and 'medieval' are in fact synonymous; to deny that art can be Christian on the pretext that Christianity stands above cultures is not to see the content and the value of this art; it is to deny elements of truth and also, thereby, of sanctity.

The Church of Peter is visible, and continuous like water; that of John—instituted on Calvary and confirmed at the sea of Tiberias—is invisible, and discontinuous like fire. John became 'brother' of Christ and 'Son' of the Virgin, and, further, he is the prophet of the Apocalypse; Peter is charged to 'feed my sheep', but his Church seems to have inherited also his denials, whence the Renaissance and its direct and indirect consequences; however, 'the gates of hell shall not prevail against it'. John 'tarries till I come', and this mystery remains closed to Peter.[1]

*

The Holy Spirit is given by Confirmation, through the medium of fire, for oil is none other than a form of liquid fire, as too is wine; the difference between Baptism and Confirmation could be defined by saying that the first has a negative—or 'negatively positive'—function, since it 'takes away' the state of the fall, while the second sacrament has a purely positive function in the sense that it 'gives' a light and a power that are divine.[2]

This transmission acquires a new 'dimension' and receives its full efficacy through the vows which correspond to the 'Gospel counsels'; these vows—true initiatic leaven—denote at the same time a death and a second birth, and they are in fact accompanied by symbolic funeral rites; the consecration of a

---

[1] It is significant that the Celtic Church, that mysterious springtime world which appeared as a sort of last prolongation of the golden age, held itself to be attached to St. John.

[2] According to Tertullian, 'the flesh is anointed that the soul may be sanctified; the flesh is signed that the soul may be fortified; the flesh is placed in shadow by the laying on of hands that the soul may be illumined by the Holy Spirit'. As for Baptism, the same author says that 'the flesh is washed that the soul may be purified'.—According to St. Dionysius, Baptism, Eucharist and Confirmation refer respectively to the ways of 'purification', 'illumination' and 'perfection'; according to others, it is Baptism which is called an 'illumination'; this clearly does not contradict the foregoing perspective, since all initiation 'illumines' by definition: the taking away of 'original sin' opens the way to a 'light' pre-existing in edenic man.

monk is a sort of burial.[1] By poverty, man severs himself from
the world; by chastity he severs himself from society; and by
obedience, he severs himself from himself.[2]

•

The whole of Christianity hangs on these words: Christ is
God. Likewise on the sacramental plane: the bread 'is' His
body, and the wine 'is' His blood.[3] There is, further, a connection between the eucharistic and the onomatologic mysteries:
the Named one is 'really present' in His Name, that is to say
He 'is' His Name.

The Eucharist is in a sense the 'central' means of grace of
Christianity; it must then express integrally what characterises
that tradition, and it does so in recapitulating not only the
mystery of Christ as such, but also its double application to the
'greater' and the 'lesser mysteries'; the wine corresponds to the
first and the bread to the second, and this is clearly shown not
only by the respective natures of the sacred elements, but also
by the following symbolic facts: the miracle of the bread is
'quantitative', in the sense that Christ multiplied what already
existed, while the miracle of the wine is 'qualitative', for Christ
conferred on the water a quality which it did not have, namely
that of wine. Or again, the body of the crucified Redeemer had
to be pierced in order that blood might flow out; blood thus
represents the inner aspect of the sacrifice, which is moreover
underlined by the fact that blood is liquid, hence 'non-formal',

---

[1] These funeral rites remind one of the symbolic cremation which,
in India, inaugurates the state of *sannyâsa*.

[2] The married man can be chaste 'in spirit and in truth', and the
same necessarily holds good for poverty and obedience, as is proved by
the example of St. Louis and other canonised monarchs. The reservation expressed by the words 'in spirit and in truth', or by the Pauline
formulation 'the letter killeth, but the spirit giveth life', has a capital
importance in the Christian perspective, but it also contains—and
moreover providentially—a 'two-edged sword'.

[3] For Clement of Alexandria, the body of Christ, or the eucharistic
bread, concerns active life or faith, and the blood or the wine,
contemplation and gnosis.

while the body is solid, hence 'formal'; the body of Christ had to be pierced because, to use the language of Meister Eckhart, 'if you want the kernel, you must break the shell'. The water which flowed from Christ's side and proved His death is like the negative aspect of the transmuted soul: it is the 'extinction' which, according to the point of view, either accompanies or precedes the beatific plenitude of the divine blood; it is the 'death' which precedes 'Life', and which is as it were its external proof.

*

Christianity hangs also on the two supreme commandments, which contain 'all the law and the prophets'. In gnosis, the first commandment—total love of God—implies awakened consciousness of the Self, while the second—love of the neighbour—refers to seeing the Self in what is 'not-I'. Likewise for the injunctions of *oratio et jejunium*: all Christianity hangs on these two disciplines, 'prayer' and 'fasting'.

Oratio et jejunium: 'Fasting' is, first, abstention from evil and next the 'void for God' (*vacare Deo*) where 'prayer'—the 'remembrance of God'—establishes itself, thus fulfilling the victory already won by the Redeemer.

'Prayer' culminates in a constant recalling of divine Names, in so far as it is a question of an articulated 'remembrance'. The Golden Legend, so rich in precious teachings, contains stories which bear witness to this: a knight wished to renounce the world and entered the Cistercian order; he was illiterate and, further, incapable of retaining, from all the teachings he received, anything but the words *Ave Maria*; these words 'he kept with such great collectedness that he pronounced them ceaselessly for himself wherever he went and whatever he was doing'. After his death, a beautiful lily grew on his grave, and on each petal was written in golden letters *Ave Maria*; the monks opened the grave and saw that the root of the lily was growing from the knight's mouth.—To this story we have only one word to add concerning the 'divine quality' of the Name of the Virgin: he who says Jesus, says God; and equally, he who says Mary, says Jesus, so that the *Ave Maria*—or the Name of Mary—is, of the divine Names, the one which is closest to man.

The Golden Legend recounts also that the executioners of St. Ignatius of Antioch were astonished by the fact that the saint pronounced the Name of Christ without ceasing: 'I cannot keep from doing so', he told them, 'for it is written in my heart.' After the saint's death, the pagans opened his heart and there saw, written in golden letters, the Name of Jesus.[1]

*

God is Love, and He is Light: but He is also, in Christ, sacrifice and suffering, and that again is an aspect or an extension of Love. Christ has two natures, divine and human, and He offers also two ways, gnosis and charity: the way of charity, in so far as it is distinguished from gnosis, implies grief, for perfect love is willing to suffer; it is in suffering that man best proves his love; but there is also in this as it were a price to be paid for the 'intellectual easiness' of such a perspective. In the way of

[1] The same fact is recounted of a Dominican saint, Catherine of Racconigi. Apart from the *Ave Maria* and the Name of Jesus, mention should be made of the double invocation *Jesu Maria*, which contains as it were two mystical dimensions, as also of *Christe eleison* which is in effect an abridgement of the 'Jesus Prayer' of the Eastern Church; it is known that the mystical science of jaculatory prayer was transmitted to the West by Cassian, who appears retrospectively as the providential intermediary between the two great branches of Christian spirituality, whilst in his own time he was, for the West, the representative of the mystical tradition as such. And let us recall here equally these liturgical words: '*Panem celestem accipiam et nomen Domini invocabo*', and: '*Calicem salutaris accipiam et nomen Domini invocabo*'.—In Greek and Slav monasteries a knotted chaplet forms part of the investiture of the Small Schema and the Great Schema: it is conferred ritually on the monk or the nun. The Superior takes the chaplet in his left hand and says: 'Take, brother N., the sword of the Spirit which is the word of God, to pray to Jesus without ceasing, for you must constantly have the Name of the Lord Jesus in the mind, in the heart and on the lips, saying: "Lord Jesus Christ, Son of God, have mercy on me, a sinner".' In the same order of ideas, we would draw attention to the 'act of love'—the perpetual prayer of the heart—revealed, in our times, to Sister Consolata of Testona. (See *Jesus Appeals to the World*. Society of St. Paul, N.Y., 1955.)

gnosis where the whole emphasis is on pure contemplation and the chief concern is with the glorious aspect of Christ rather than with his grievous humanity—and there is in certain respects a participation in the divine nature, which is ever blissful and immutable—suffering is not imposed in the same way; that is, it does not, in principle, have to exceed the exigencies of a general ascesis, such as the Gospel designates by the term *jejunium*; a quasi-impersonal detachment here takes precedence over individual desire for sacrifice. All Christian spirituality oscillates between these two poles, although the aspect of charity-suffering greatly preponderates, in practice—and for obvious reasons—over the aspect gnosis-contemplation.

The question: 'What is God?' or: 'What am I?' outweighs, in the soul of the gnostic, the question: 'What does God want of me?' or: 'What must I do?' although these questions are far from being irrelevant, since man is always man. The gnostic, who sees God 'everywhere and nowhere', does not first of all base himself on alternatives outside himself, although he cannot escape them; what matters to him above all is that the world is everywhere woven of the same existential qualities and poses in all circumstances the same problems of remoteness and proximity.

*

The insistence, in the Christian climate, on the virtue of humility—or rather the manner of this insistence or of the display of this virtue—leads us to return to this problem, which is at once moral and mystical.[1]

Humility has two aspects prefigured in the Gospels, one by the washing of the feet and the other by the cry of abandonment on the cross. The first humility is effacement: when we are brought, rightly or wrongly, to see a quality in ourselves, we must first attribute it to God and secondly see in ourselves either the limits of this quality, or defects that could neutralise it; and when we are brought to see a defect in others, we must

[1] We have already spoken of it in our *Spiritual Perspectives and Human Facts* (Faber 1954) towards the end of the book.

first try to find its trace or the responsibility for it in ourselves and secondly force ourselves to discover qualities which can compensate it. But truth—provided it is within our reach—surpasses every other value, so that to submit to truth is the best way to be humble; virtue is good because it is true, and not inversely. Christ humiliated Himself in washing the feet of His disciples. He abased Himself by serving while He was the Master, but not by calumniating Himself; He did not say: 'I am worse than you,' and He gave no example of virtue to contradict truth or intelligence.[1]

The second—the great—humility is spiritual death, the 'losing of life' for God, the extinction of the *ego*; this is what saints have had in view in describing themselves as 'the greatest of sinners'; if this expression has a meaning, it applies to the *ego* as such, and not to such and such an *ego*. Since all sin comes from the *ego* and since without it there would be no sin, it is indeed the *ego* which is the 'most vile' or the 'lowest of sinners'; when the contemplative has identified his 'I' with the principle of individuation, he perceives as it were in himself the root of all sin and the very principle of evil; it is as if he had assumed, after the example of Christ, all our imperfections, in order to dissolve them in himself, in the light of God and in the burnings of love. For a St. Benedict or a St. Bernard, the 'degrees of humility' are stages in the extinction of the passionate 'I', stages marked by attitude-symbols, disciplines which further the transmutation of the soul; the key to this wisdom is that Christ was humiliated on the cross through identifying Himself, in the

---

[1] Christ gave other teachings on humility, for example when He said that He had not come to be served but to serve, or when He said that 'whosoever . . . shall humble himself as this little child, the same is the greatest in the kingdom of heaven'; now the true nature of all children is purity and simplicity, not rivalry. Let us recall also the parable of the uppermost rooms at feasts.—According to St. Thomas Aquinas, humility demands neither that we should submit what is divine in us to what is divine in another, nor that we should submit what is human in us to what is human in another; still less has the divine to submit to the human; but there is still the question, sometimes delicate but never insoluble, of the right definition of things.

night of abandonment, with the night of the human *ego*, and not through identifying Himself with such and such an 'I'; He felt Himself forsaken, not because He was Jesus, but because He had become man as such; He had to cease being Jesus that He might taste all the straitness, all the separation from God, of the pure *ego* and thereby of our state of fall.[1]

That we may not be able to determine our place in the hierarchy of sinners by no means signifies that we have not the certainty of being 'vile', not only as *ego* in general, but also, and therefore, as a particular *ego*; to believe oneself 'vile' for the sole reason that one is 'I' would empty humility of its content.

Humility, in Christianity, is conceived with reference to love, and this is one of the factors conferring on it its characteristic texture. 'The love of God', says St. Augustine, 'comprises all the virtues.'

*

'And the light shineth in darkness; and the darkness comprehended it not.' The message of Christ, by its form, is addressed *a priori* to the passional element in man, to the point of fall in his nature, but it remains gnostic or sapiential in Christ Himself and therefore in trinitarian metaphysics, not to speak of the sapiential symbolism of Christ's teachings and parables. But it is in relation to the general form—the volitional perspective— of the message that Christ could say: 'They that are whole have no need of the physician, but they that are sick: I came not to call the righteous, but sinners to repentance' (Mark ii, 17). Again, when Christ says 'Judge not, that ye be not judged', He is referring to our passional nature and not to pure intelligence,

[1] The saying of Christ: 'Why callest thou me good? There is none good but one, that is, God:' belongs to the greater humility we have here in view; it is the same when Christ cites little children as examples.—If it were necessary to take literally the mystic's conviction of being the 'vilest of sinners', it would not be possible to explain how saints who had had this conviction could speak evil of some heretic; moreover it would be absurd to ask men to have an acute sense of the least defects of their nature and at the same time to be incapable of discerning these defects in another.

which is neutral and is identified with those 'that are whole'. If Christ shall come to 'judge the quick and the dead', that is again a matter of the Intellect—which alone has the right to judge—and of the equating of Christ and Intellect.

The volitional perspective, to which we have just alluded, is affirmed in the clearest possible way in biblical history: we see there a people at once passionate and mystical struggling in the grip of a Law which crushes and fascinates it, and this prefigures, in a providential way, the struggles of the passional soul—of every soul in so far as it is subject to passions—with the truth which is the final end of the human state. The Bible always speaks of 'that which happens' and almost never of 'that which is', though it does so implicitly as the Kabbalists point out; we are the first to recognise this, but it alters nothing in the visible nature of these Scriptures, nor in the human causes behind this nature. From another angle, Judaism had hidden what Christianity was called on to make openly manifest[1]; in turn, the Jews had openly manifested, from the moral point of view, what Christians, later, learnt to hide; the ancient crudity was replaced by an esotericism of love, no doubt, but also by a new hypocrisy.

It is necessary to take account equally of this: the volitional perspective has a tendency to retain the *ego* because of the idea of moral responsibility, while gnosis, on the contrary, tends to reduce it to the cosmic powers of which it is a combination and an outcome. And again: from the point of view of will and passion, men are equal; but they are not so from the point of view of pure intellection, for the latter introduces into man an element of the absolute which, as such, exceeds him infinitely. To the moralising question: 'Who art thou that judgest another?'—a question by which some would like to obliterate

---

[1] The commentators of the Torah state that the impediment of speech from which Moses suffered was imposed on him by God so that he should not be able to divulge the Mysteries which, precisely, the Law of Sinai had to veil and not to unveil; but these Mysteries were, basically, none other than the 'Christ-given Mysteries'.

all 'wisdom of serpents' or all 'discerning of spirits' in a vague
and would-be charitable psychologism—to this question one
would have the right to reply 'God' in every case of infallible
judgement; for intelligence, in so far as it is 'relatively absolute',
escapes the jurisdiction of virtue, and consequently its rights
surpass those of man regarded as passional and fallible *ego*; God
is in the truth of every truth. The saying that 'no one can be
judge and party in his own cause' could be applied to the *ego*
only in so far as the latter limits or darkens the mind, for it is
arbitrary to attribute in principle to the intelligence as such a
limit with respect to an order of contingencies; to assert, as
certain moralists would, that man has no right to judge, amounts
to saying that he has no intelligence, that he is only will or
passion and that he has no kind of likeness to God.

The sacred rights of the Intellect appear besides in the fact
that Christians have not been able to dispense with the wisdom
of Plato, and that, later, the Latins found the need for recourse
to Aristotelianism, as if thereby recognising that *religio* could
not do without the element of wisdom, which a too exclusive
perspective of love had allowed to fall into discredit.[1] But if
knowledge is a profound need of the human spirit, it is by that
very fact also a way.

To return to our earlier thought, we could also express ourselves thus: contrary to what is the case in gnosis, love scarcely
has the right to judge another; it takes all upon itself and excuses
everything, at least on the level where it is active, a level the
limits of which vary according to individual natures; 'pious
fraud'[2]—out of charity—is the price of volitional individualism.

[1] The ancient tendency to reduce *sophia* to a 'philosophy', an 'art
for art's sake' or a 'knowledge without love', hence a pseudo-wisdom,
has necessitated the predominance, in Christianity, of the contrary
viewpoint. Love, in the sapiential perspective, is the element which
surpasses simple ratiocination and makes knowledge effective; this
cannot be insisted on too much.

[2] Veracity, which in the end has more importance than moral con-
jectures, implies in short the consequent use of logic, that is to say:
to put nothing higher than truth, nor to fall into the contrary fault
of believing that to be impartial means not to consider anyone right

If gnosis, for its part, discerns essentially—and on all levels—both spirits and values, this is because its point of view is never personal, so that in gnosis the distinction between 'me' and 'other', and the subtle and paradoxical obstinacies attaching to this, scarcely have meaning; but here too, the application of the principle depends on the limitations imposed on us by the nature of things and of ourselves.

Charity with regard to our neighbour, when it is the act of a direct consciousness and not just of a moral sentiment, implies seeing ourselves in the other and the other in ourselves; the scission between *ego* and *alter* must be overcome, that the cleavage between Heaven and earth may be healed.

*

According to St. Thomas, it is not in the nature of free will to choose evil, although this possibility derives from having freedom of agency associated with a fallible creature. Will and liberty are thus connected; the Doctor, that is, introduces into the will an intellectual element and makes the will, quite properly, participate in intelligence. Will does not cease to be will by choosing evil—we have already said this on other occasions—but it ceases fundamentally to be free, and so intellective; in the first case, it is the dynamic faculty, power of the passions—animals also have a will—and in the second, the dynamisation of discernment. It could be added that neither does intelligence cease to be itself when in error, but in this case the relationship is less direct than for the will; the Holy Spirit (Will, Love) 'is delegated' by the Son (Intellect, Knowledge) and not inversely.

Christian doctrine does not claim that moral effort produces

or wrong. One must not stifle discernment for the sake of impartiality, for objectivity consists, not in absolving the wrong or accusing the right, but in seeing things as they are, whether that pleases us or not: it is, consequently, to have a sense of proportion as much as a sense of subtlety of degrees. It would be useless to say such elementary things if one did not meet at every turn this false virtue which distorts the exact vision of facts but could dispense with its scruples if only it realised sufficiently the value and efficacy of humility before God.

metaphysical knowledge, but it does teach that the restoring of the fallen will—the extirpation of the passions—releases the contemplative power latent in the depths of our theomorphic nature; this contemplative power is like a window on which the divine Light cannot but fall, whether as Justice or still more as Mercy; in gnosis, this process of mystical alchemy is accompanied by appropriate concepts and states of consciousness.[1] Seen from this angle, the primacy of love is not opposed to the perspective of wisdom, but illumines its operative aspect.[2]

*

The morality which offers the other cheek—so far as morality can here be spoken of—means not an unwonted solicitude towards one's adversary, but complete indifference towards the fetters of this world, or more precisely a refusal to let oneself be caught up in the vicious circle of terrestrial causations. The

---

[1] Knowledge is then 'sanctifying' and is not limited to satisfying some more or less justifiable needs of causality; it accords fully with St. Paul's doctrine of charity. The implacability of such knowledge is not arrogance but purity. Gnosis makes of knowledge something effective, ontological, 'lived'. Outside of gnosis, it is a question not of extirpating the passions, but of directing them towards Heaven.

[2] The Augustinian and Platonic doctrine of knowledge is still in perfect accord with gnosis, while Thomist and Aristotelian sensualism, without being false on its own level and within its own limits, accords with the exigencies of the way of love, in the specific sense of the term *bhakti*. But this reservation is far from applying to the whole of Thomism, which identifies itself, in many respects, with truth unqualified.—It is necessary to reject the opinion of those who believe that Thomism, or any other ancient wisdom, has an effective value only when we 're-create it in ourselves'—we, 'men of today'!—and that if St. Thomas had read Descartes, Kant and the philosophers of the nineteenth and twentieth centuries, he would have expressed himself differently; in reality, he would then only have had to refute a thousand errors the more. If an ancient saying is right, there is nothing to do but accept it; if it is false, there is no reason to take notice of it; but to want to 'rethink' it through a veil of new errors or impressions quite clearly has no interest, and any such attempt merely shows the degree to which the sense of intrinsic and timeless truth has been lost.

man who wants to be right at any price on the personal plane, loses serenity and moves away from the 'one thing needful'; the affairs of this world bring with them only disturbances, and disturbances take one farther from God. But peace, like every spiritual attitude, can be independent from external activity; holy anger is internally calm, and when to execute judgement is an unavoidable task—unavoidable because motivated by higher and nonpersonal interests—it is quite compatible with a mind free from attachment and hatred. Christ fights against passions and personal interest, but not against the performance of duty or the collective interest; in other words, He is opposed to personal interest when the latter is passionate or harmful to the interests of others, and He condemns hatred, even when it serves a higher interest.

The 'non-violence' advocated by the Gospels symbolises—and makes effective—the virtue of the mind preoccupied with 'what is' rather than with 'what happens'. As a rule, man loses much time and energy in questioning himself about the injustice of his fellows as well as about supposed hardships of destiny; whether there be human injustice or divine punishment, the world—the 'current of forms' or the 'cosmic wheel'—is what it is, it simply follows its course; it is conformable to its own nature. Men cannot not be unjust, seeing that they form part of this current; to be detached from the current and to act contrary to the logic of facts and of the slaveries which it engenders is bound to appear as madness in the eyes of the world, but it is, in reality, to adopt here below the point of view of eternity. And to adopt this point of view is to see oneself from very far away: it is to see that we ourselves form part of this world of injustice, and that is one reason the more for remaining indifferent amid the uproar of human quarrelling. The saint is the man who acts as if he had died and returned to life; having already ceased to be 'himself', in the earthly sense, he has absolutely no intention of returning to that dream, but maintains himself in a kind of wakefulness that the world, with its narrowness and impurities, cannot understand.

Pure love is not of this world of oppositions; it is by origin celestial and its end is God; it lives, as it were in itself, by its own light and in the ray of God-Love, and that is why charity 'seeketh not her own, is not easily provoked, thinketh no evil; rejoiceth not in iniquity, but rejoiceth in the truth; beareth all things, believeth all things, hopeth all things, endureth all things' (1 Cor. xiii, 5–7).

Mysteries of Christ
and of the Virgin

God became man, that man might become God. The first mystery is the Incarnation, the second is the Redemption.

However, just as the Word, in assuming flesh, was already in a sense crucified, so too man, in returning to God, must share in both mysteries: the *ego* is crucified to the world, but the grace of salvation is made incarnate in the heart; sanctity is the birth and life of Christ in us.

This mystery of the Incarnation has two aspects: the Word on the one hand and His human receptacle on the other; Christ and the Virgin-Mother. To be able to realise this mystery in itself, the soul must be like the Virgin; for just as the sun can be reflected in water only when it is calm, so the soul can receive Christ only in virginal purity, in original simplicity, and not in sin, which is turmoil and unbalance.

By 'mystery' we do not mean something incomprehensible in principle—unless it be on the purely rational level—but something which flows out into the Infinite, or which is envisaged in this respect, so that intelligibility becomes limitless and humanly inexhaustible. A mystery is always 'something of God'.

*

Ave Maria gratia plena, dominus tecum: benedicta tu in mulieribus, et benedictus fructus ventris tui, Jesus.[1]

Maria is the purity, the beauty, the goodness and the humility of the cosmic Substance; the microcosmic reflection

[1] 'The devotion of the Rosary . . . is, when correctly grasped, as ancient as the Church. It is the appropriate devotion of Christians. It serves to revive and maintain the spirit and life of Christianity. The novelty of the name can offend only those who do not know its real sense: and St. Dominic, who is regarded as the Author of this devotion is in effect only its Restorer.' (*La solide Dévotion du Rosaire*, by an unknown Dominican of the beginning of the eighteenth century.)

of this Substance is the soul in a state of grace. The soul in the state of baptismal grace corresponds to the Virgin Mary; the blessing of the Virgin is on him who purifies his soul for God. This purity—the Marial state—is the essential condition, not only for the reception of the sacraments, but also for the spiritual actualisation of the real Presence of the Word. By the word *ave*, the soul expresses the idea that, in conforming to the perfection of Substance, it puts itself at the same time in connection with it, whilst imploring the help of the Virgin Mary, who personifies this perfection.

Gratia plena: primordial Substance, by reason of its purity, its goodness and its beauty, is filled with the divine Presence. It is pure, because it contains nothing other than God; it is good, because it compensates and absorbs all forms of cosmic disequilibrium, for it is totality and therefore equilibrium; it is beautiful, because it is totally submissive to God. It is thus that the soul, the microcosmic reflection of Substance—corrupted by the fall—must again become pure, good and beautiful.

Dominus tecum: this Substance is not only filled with the divine Presence in an ontological or existential manner, in the sense that it is penetrated with it by definition, that is to say by its very nature, but it is also constantly communicating with the Word as such. So, if *gratia plena* means that the divine Mystery is immanent in the Substance as such, *Dominus tecum* signifies that God, in His metacosmic transcendence, is revealed to the Substance, just as the eye, which is filled with light, sees in addition the sun itself. The soul filled with grace will see God.

Benedicta tu in mulieribus: compared with all secondary substances, the total Substance alone is perfect, and totally under the divine Grace. All substances derive from it by a rupture of equilibrium; equally, all fallen souls derive from the primordial soul through the fall. The soul in a state of grace, the soul pure, good and beautiful, regains primordial perfection; it is, thereby, 'blessed among all' microcosmic substances.

Et benedictus fructus ventris tui, Jesus: that which, in principle, is *Dominus tecum*, becomes, in manifestation, *fructus ventris tui,*

Jesus: that is to say that the Word which communicates with the ever-virgin substance of the total Creation, is reflected in an inverse sense within this Creation: it will there appear as the fruit, the result, not as the root, the cause. And again: the soul submissive to God by its purity, its goodness and its beauty, seems to give birth to God, according to appearances; but this God being born in it will transmute and absorb it, as Christ transmutes and absorbs His mystical body, the Church, which from being militant and suffering becomes triumphant. But in reality, the Word is not born in the Substance, for the Word is immutable; it is the Substance which dies in the Word. Again, when God seems to germinate in the soul, it is in reality the soul which dies in God. *Benedictus:* the Word which becomes incarnate is itself Benediction; nevertheless, since according to appearances it is manifest as Substance, as soul it is called blessed; for it is then envisaged, not in respect of its trans-cendence—which would render Substance unreal—but in respect of its appearance, its Incarnation: *fructus*.

Jesus: the Word which determines Substance, reveals itself to the latter. Macrocosmically, it is the Word which mani-fests itself in the Universe as the divine Spirit; microcosmically, it is the Real Presence affirming itself at the centre of the soul, radiating outwards and finally transmuting and absorbing it.[1]

*

The virginal perfections are purity, beauty, goodness and humility; it is these qualities which the soul in quest of God must realise.

Purity: the soul is empty of all desire. Every natural move-ment which asserts itself in the soul is then considered in respect of its passional quality, its aspect of concupiscence, of seduction. This perfection is cold, hard and transparent like a diamond. It is immortality excluding all corruption.

[1] This expression should not be taken quite literally any more than other expressions of union which will follow; here, what is essential is to be aware of 'deification', whatever significance one may give to this term.

Beauty: the beauty of the Virgin expresses divine Peace. It is in the perfect equilibrium of its possibilities that the universal Substance realises its beauty. In this perfection, the soul quits all dissipation to repose in its own substantial, primordial, ontological perfection. We said above that the soul must be like a perfectly calm expanse of water; every natural movement of the soul will then appear as agitation, dissipation, shrivelling up, and so as ugliness.

Goodness: the mercy of the cosmic Substance consists in this, that, virgin in relation to its products, it comprises an inexhaustible power of equilibrium, of setting aright, of healing, of absorbing evil and of manifesting good; being maternal towards beings who address themselves to it, it in no way refuses them its assistance. Likewise, the soul must divert its love from the hardened *ego* and direct it towards the neighbour and the whole of creation; the distinction between 'I' and 'other' is as if abolished, the 'I' has become 'other' and the 'other' become 'I'. The passional distinction between 'I' and 'thou' is a state of death, comparable to the separation between the soul and God.

Humility: the Virgin, despite her supreme sanctity, remains woman and aspires to no other role; the humble soul is conscious of its own rank and effaces itself before what surpasses it. It is thus that the *Materia Prima* of the Universe remains on its own level and never seeks to appropriate to itself the transcendence of the Principle.

The mysteries, joyous, grievous and glorious of Mary are so many aspects of cosmic reality on the one hand, and of mystical life on the other.

Like Mary—and like universal Substance—the sanctified soul is 'virgin', 'spouse', and 'mother'.

*

The nature of Christ appears in four mysteries: incarnation, love, sacrifice, divinity; and in these the human soul must participate in diverse ways.

The incarnation: this is manifested, as principle, in every positive divine act, such as creation, or, within creation, in the different affirmations of the Divine, such as the Scriptures. In the soul, it is the birth of the Divine in us, grace, but also gnosis, which transforms man and gives him salvation; equally, it is the divine act of Prayer of the Heart, the Name of God made incarnate in the soul as an invisible force. Christ, as pure divine affirmation, enters the world—and the soul—with the force of lightning, of the drawn sword; all natural imagery of the soul appears then as a passivity or a complacency towards the world, a forgetfulness of God out of weakness and negligence. The incarnation is, in the soul, the victorious—and ceaselessly renewed—presence of the divine Miracle.

Love: God is love, infinite life. The *ego* on the contrary is a state of death, comparable, in its congenital self-centredness, to a stone, and also, in its paltriness, to sterile and shifting sand. The hardened heart must be liquefied; its indifference towards God must turn into fervour, while thereby it becomes indifferent as regards the *ego* and the world. The gift of tears is one manifestation of this liquefaction; spiritual intoxication is another.

Sacrifice: on the cross, the annihilation of Christ attains its culminating point in the state of abandonment between Heaven and earth. It is thus that the *ego* must be annihilated, in a perfect void, before the exclusive Reality of God.

Divinity: that which corresponds to it in the soul is pure spirituality, that is to say permanent union with God. It is the remembrance of God which must become the true centre of our being, in place of the illusory *ego* which dissipates itself in the appearances of this world below. The human person becomes perfectly 'itself' only beyond itself, in profound and inexpressible Union.

*

The Lord's Prayer is the most excellent prayer of all, since it has Christ for its author; it is, therefore, more excellent, as a prayer, than the *Ave*, and that is why it is the first prayer of the

Rosary. But the *Ave* is more excellent than the Lord's Prayer in that it contains the Name of Christ, mysteriously identified with Christ Himself, since 'God and His Name are one'. Christ is more than the Prayer He taught, and the *Ave*, which contains Christ through His Name, is thus more than this Prayer; this is why the recitations of the *Ave* are much more numerous than those of the *Pater*, and why the *Ave* constitutes, with the Name of the Lord that it contains, the very substance of the Rosary. What we have just stated amounts to saying that the prayer of the 'servant' addressed to the 'Lord' corresponds to the 'Lesser Mysteries'—and we recall that these concern the realisation of the primordial or edenic state, and hence the fullness of the human state—while the Name of God itself corresponds to the 'Great Mysteries', the finality of which is beyond all individual states.

From the microcosmic point of view, as we have seen, 'Mary' is the soul in the state of 'sanctifying grace', qualified to receive the 'Real Presence'; 'Jesus' is the divine Seed, the 'Real Presence' which must bring about the transmutation of the soul, namely its universalisation, or its reintegration in the Eternal. 'Mary'—like the 'Lotus'—is 'surface' or 'horizontal'; 'Jesus'—like the 'Jewel'[1]—is 'centre' and, in the dynamic relationship, 'vertical'. 'Jesus' is God in us, God who penetrates us and transfigures us.

Among the meditations of the Rosary, the 'joyous Mysteries' concern, from the point of view adopted here, and in connection with jaculatory prayers, the 'Real Presence' of the Divine in the human; as for the 'grievous Mysteries', they describe the redemptive 'imprisonment' of the Divine in the human, the inevitable profanation of the 'Real Presence' by human limitations; finally, the 'glorious Mysteries' relate to the victory of the Divine over the human, the freeing of the soul by the Spirit.

[1] We are here alluding to the well-known Buddhist formula: *Om mani padmê hum*. There is an analogy worth noticing between this formula and the name 'Jesus of Nazareth': the literal meaning of *Nazareth* is 'flower', and *mani padmê* means 'jewel in the lotus'.

Of the Cross

If the Incarnation has the significance of a 'descent' of God, Christ is also equivalent to the whole of creation. He contains it, as it were; He is a second creation which purifies and redeems the first. He assumes, with the cross, the evil of Existence; to be able to assume this evil, it was necessary that God should become Existence. The cross is everywhere because creation is of necessity separated from God; Existence affirms itself and blossoms out through joy, but the latter becomes sin to the extent that God is not its object, although all joy contains a metaphysical justification from the fact that it is directed to God by its very nature as existent; every sin is broken at the foot of the cross. But man is not made solely of blind desire; he has received intelligence that he may know God; he must become conscious of the divine end in everything, and at the same time he must 'take up his cross' and 'offer the other cheek', that is to say escape from the internal logic of the prison of existence; his logic, which is 'madness' in the eyes of the world, must transcend the plane of this prison, it must be 'vertical' or celestial, not 'horizontal' or terrestrial.

Existence or 'manifestation' has two aspects: the tree and the cross; the tree, joyous in Eden but bearing the serpent, and the grievous cross carrying the Word made flesh. For the impious, Existence is a world of passion that man would justify by philosophy 'according to the flesh'; for the elect, it is a world of trial transpierced by grace, faith, gnosis.

Jesus is not only the new Adam, but also the new Creation. The old is totality and circumference, the new, unicity and centre.

*

We can no more escape the cross than we can escape Existence. At the root of all that exists, there is the cross. The *ego* is a propensity drawing man away from God; the cross is a halting of that propensity. If Existence is 'something of God', it is also something 'which is not God', and it is this which the *ego* incarnates. The cross brings the latter back to the former and in so doing makes possible the conquest of Existence.

What makes the problem of Existence so complex is that God shines through everywhere, since nothing could exist outside of Him; all depends on never being separated from this distant perception of the Divine. And that is why joy in the shadow of the cross is conceivable and even inevitable; to exist is to experience joy, even though it be at the foot of the cross. That is where man must keep himself, since such is the profound nature of things; man can violate this nature only in appearance. Suffering and death are none other than the cross reappearing in the cosmic flesh; Existence is a rose signed with a cross.

*

Social morals distinguish between the rightness of one man and the wrongness of another; but the mystical morals of Christ, strictly speaking, admit no one to be right, or rather, they are situated on a plane where no one is entirely right, since every man is a sinner and 'there is none good but one, that is, God'.[1] The Law of Moses has a man stoned for wronging society, an adulterer for example, but for Christ there is only God who can be wronged and this excludes all forms of vengeance; every man is guilty before the Eternal. Every sin is that of Adam and Eve, and every human being is Adam or Eve[2]; the first act of justice will then be to forgive our neighbour. The fault of 'the

[1] 'For I know nothing by myself; yet am I not hereby justified: but he that judgeth me is the Lord' (1 Cor. iv, 4).

[2] St. Gregory the Great says in a letter, quoted by the Venerable Bede in his *Ecclesiastical History of the English Nation*, that 'every sin proceeds from three causes, namely suggestion, pleasure and consent. Suggestion comes from the devil, pleasure from the body and consent from the will. The serpent suggested the first sin, and Eve, as flesh, found in it a carnal pleasure, while Adam, as mind, consented to it; but only the most subtle intelligence can discern between suggestion and pleasure, and between pleasure and consent. . . .'

other' is at bottom our own; it is only a manifestation of the latent fault which constitutes our common substance.

But Christ, whose Kingdom is 'not of this world', leaves open a door for human justice so far as it is inevitable: 'Render . . . unto Caesar the things which are Caesar's.' To deny this justice on every plane would amount to setting up injustice; however, it is necessary to overcome hatred by bringing evil back to its total root, to that 'offence' which must needs come, and above all by discovering it in our own nature, which is that of every *ego*; the *ego* is an optical illusion which makes a mote out of a beam, and conversely, according to whether it is a question of 'ourselves' or of 'another'. It is necessary to find, through the Truth, that serenity which understands all, 'forgives all', and reduces all to equilibrium; it is necessary to conquer evil with the peace which being beyond evil is not its contrary; true peace has no contrary.

'He that is without sin among you, let him first cast a stone': we are all of a same sinful substance, a same matter susceptible to this abscess, evil, and we are, in consequence, all joint partners in evil, in a way that is doubtless indirect but none the less real; it is as if everyone carried in himself a particle of responsibility for all sin. Sin then appears as a cosmic accident, exactly as is the *ego* on a larger scale; strictly speaking, he is without sin who is without *ego* and who, thereby, is as the wind of which no man can 'tell whence it cometh, and whither it goeth'. If God alone has the right to punish, it is because He is beyond the *ego*; hatred means to arrogate to oneself the place of God, to forget one's human sharing of a common misery, to attribute to one's own 'I' a kind of absoluteness, detaching it from that substance of which individuals are only so many contractions or knots. It is true that God sometimes delegates his right of punishment to man in so far as he rises above the 'I', or must and can so rise; but to be the instrument of God is to be without hatred against man. In hatred, man forgets 'original sin' and thereby loads himself, in a certain sense, with the sin of the other; it is because we make God of ourselves whenever we hate, that we must love our enemies. To hate another is to forget that God alone is perfect and that God alone is Judge. In good logic one can hate only 'in God' and 'for God'; we must hate the *ego*, not the 'immortal soul', and hate him who hates God, and not otherwise, which amounts to saying that we should hate his hatred of God and not his soul. Likewise, when Christ says that it is necessary to 'hate' one's 'father and mother', that means that it is necessary to reject whatever in them is 'against God', that is to say their character of attachment and their function as obstacle in respect of 'the one thing needful'. Such 'hatred' implies for those whom it concerns a virtual liberation; it is then, on the plane of eschatological realities, an act of love.

*

'To bear the cross' is to keep oneself close to the cross of existence. Existence has the pole 'sin' and the pole 'cross', the blind launching into enjoyment and the conscious stopping; the 'broad way' and the 'narrow way'. To 'bear the cross' is, essentially, not to 'swim with the tide'; it is to 'discern spirits', to keep oneself, incorruptible, in this apparent nothingness which is the Truth. To 'bear the cross' means then to endure this nothingness, threshold of God; and since the world is pride, egoism, passion and false knowledge, it means to be humble and charitable, to 'die' and be 'as a little child'. This nothingness becomes suffering in proportion as we are pride and so, by this fact, it makes us suffer; the fire of purgatory is nothing else: it is our substance which burns, not because God wishes to hurt us, but because it is what it is; because it is 'of this world' and in proportion to its being so.

*

The cross is the divine fissure through which Mercy flows from the Infinite.

The centre of the cross, where the two dimensions intersect, is the mystery of forsakenness: it is the 'spiritual moment' when the soul loses itself, when it 'is no more' and when it 'is not yet'.

Like the whole Passion of Christ, this cry is not only a mystery
of grief in which man must share by renunciation, but also, on
the contrary, an 'opening' that God alone could effect, and
which He did effect because He was God; and that is why 'my
yoke is easy, and my burden is light'. The victory which devolves
on man has already been won by Jesus; for man nothing remains
but to open himself to this victory, which thus becomes his own.

*

What is 'abstraction' with the logician becomes as it were
corporeal with the Word made flesh. The spear of the centurion
Longinus has just pierced Christ's side; a drop of divine blood,
flowing down the spear, touches the man's hand. At that
moment, the world collapses for him like a house of glass,
the darkness of existence is torn away, his soul becomes like
a weeping wound. He is as if drunk, but with a drunkenness that
is cold and pure; his whole life is henceforth like an echo
repeating a thousand times that single instant at the foot of the
cross. He has just been reborn, not because he has 'understood'
the Truth, but because the Truth has seized him existentially
and torn him, with a 'concrete' gesture, from this world. The
Word made flesh is the Truth become matter as it were, but
at the same time a matter transfigured and new-minted, a
matter which is burning light, transforming and delivering.